CW01651623

Special Exhibition Adult
27 Oct 2017
£ 6,00
POS CASTLE FRON 523 928

Rembrandt: Lightening the Darkness

Giorgia Bottinelli & Francesca Vanke
Norfolk Museums Service

Acknowledgments

Our first thanks go to Birketts for sponsoring our exhibition *Rembrandt: Lightening the Darkness* (21 October 2017 - 7 January 2018) and to the John Jarrold Trust for supporting the creation of a 'print studio' within the exhibition and our programme of demonstrations and workshops. We are very grateful to Amanda Geitner and Angela Dunn at East Anglia Art Fund for championing both our exhibition and publication so thoroughly. Without their support, this project would not have been possible.

We have been very fortunate to receive considerable support from the British Museum, National Galleries of Scotland, National Gallery and Royal Collection, who lent precious paintings, drawings and prints by Rembrandt to our exhibition. We are indebted to Sarah A.M. Turner for supplying essential information about Percy Moore Turner; to Erik Hinterding, Curator of Prints at the Rijksmuseum, Amsterdam for his invaluable advice and expertise; and to An Van Camp and Andrew Wood for contributing to this publication.

Among the colleagues who worked hard to realise this project, we would particularly like to thank Fi Hitchcock, who coordinated all aspects of exhibition organisation; Lucy McNeill, who produced stunning new images of our Rembrandt holdings; Sarah Norcross-Robinson, who oversaw the conservation work needed; and Lynne Avery-Johnson for her inspiring exhibition design.

Giorgia Bottinelli
and Francesca Vanke

Published by Norfolk Museums Service 2017
All images © Norfolk Museums Service

No part of this catalogue may be reproduced, stored in a retrieval system or transmitted in any form or by any means, electronic, mechanical, photocopying, recording or otherwise without the permission of the publishers.

ISBN: 978-0903101899

Designed by Steve Hayes
Printed by Lamport Gilbert

Inside cover: **Canal with a large Boat and Bridge ('Het schuytje op de voorgrond') (II/II)**, 1650
Etching and drypoint on paper
8.2 x 10.7 cm
Signed and dated in plate lower left of subject 'Rembrandt f. 1650'
NWHCM : 1951.47.52

Birketts Clear Legal Advice · EAST ANGLIA ART FUND Great Art for Our Region · JARROLD The John Jarrold Trust · Supported using public funding by ARTS COUNCIL ENGLAND · Norfolk Museums Service · Norwich Castle Museum & Art Gallery

Contents

Foreword

As Honorary Dutch Consul for East Anglia I am privileged to be invited to write the foreword to this book accompanying a major exhibition celebrating Norwich Castle Museum & Art Gallery's nationally important collection of Rembrandt's etchings. The exhibition is a rare and welcome chance to see the UK's fourth largest collection of Rembrandt's prints.

My role since December 2016 has been to promote a trade and cultural bridge between East Anglia and the Netherlands, which with the UK's impending departure from the EU, post Brexit, will become ever more vital.

Norfolk welcomed HE Simon Smits the Dutch Ambassador to open the exhibition. The Ambassador's visit showed him Norfolk's long historic and geographical links with the Netherlands. Supportive of the Protestant Lowlanders' uprising against their Spanish ruler, as early as 1565 Queen Elizabeth I invited the Dutch- and French-speaking Lowlanders, or 'Strangers', to come to Norwich, proclaiming them 'England's most ancient and familiar neighbours'.

These economic immigrants helped resurrect Norwich's cloth and wool industry and shaped the religious and social fabric of the City. By Rembrandt's time, at least one third of Norwich's population was of Dutch origin. Some of their descendants were Puritans who left Norwich and settled in Leiden before emigrating to America. Many noted Americans had Norwich Dutch ancestors, including Benjamin Franklin.

In 1634 Rembrandt painted Johannes Elison, Minister of the Dutch Church in Norwich and his wife Maria; the two full-length portraits were commissioned by their son, a wealthy merchant, when his parents visited him in Amsterdam. In the Netherlands as in England, such portraits, in paint or print, established social standing. Rembrandt's prints would have been known, and probably displayed, in contemporary Norwich.

In past centuries ease of travel between Norfolk and its nearest European neighbour (one day by sea from Yarmouth to Nieweport as opposed to four to London by road) enabled free interchange of people, ideas and trade. Business and cultural connections continue today through Norwich International Airport's daily KLM flights to Schiphol, KLM Engineering's centre at the Airport, Unilever's Colman's food factory, Great Yarmouth and its new Outer Harbour (built by the Dutch), offshore wind and energy industries and other shipping links across the southern North Sea. There are strong farming ties as well as academic research links: UEA is associated through Aurora with the Free University of Amsterdam, and Norwich Research Park has agricultural, food and medical connections with Dutch organisations.

These links, with roots going back to Rembrandt's day and beyond, mark the strength of the ongoing Anglo-Dutch relationship. As Lord Burghley, Elizabeth I's adviser, said of Anglo-Dutch relations: 'the one cannot live well without the friendship of the other'.

Andrew Wood
Honorary Dutch Consul for
the East of England
October 2017

Rembrandt in Norwich
Preface

In 1951 almost one hundred prints attributed to the greatest Dutch artist of all time, Rembrandt, entered the collections of Norwich Castle Museum & Art Gallery. This outstanding group of etchings and drypoints was bequeathed by Percy Moore Turner (1877-1950), an art dealer in Paris and London who left parts of his collection to various institutions in the United Kingdom and France. Thanks to Turner's generosity, Norfolk now holds the fourth most important collection of Rembrandt prints in the country after the British Museum (London), the Ashmolean Museum of Art and Archaeology (Oxford) and the Fitzwilliam Museum (Cambridge). *Rembrandt: Lightening the Darkness* is a celebration of Turner's exceptional collection and the majority of the Rembrandt works on display have been selected from his bequest. Ninety-three etchings and drypoints from Norwich's own collection are cleverly paired with a handful of loans including prints, drawings and paintings from the British Museum, the National Gallery, the Royal Collection and the National Galleries of Scotland.

The prints bequeathed by Percy Moore Turner are characterised by their high quality and include very fine early impressions. Some have been retouched in pen and ink, possibly by Rembrandt himself, and it is tempting to imagine that these impressions were proofs adapted by the Dutch master in order to improve the composition or to add more shading. Rembrandt was a perfectionist who kept reworking his copper plates and many impressions of these intermediary and unfinished stages of the plate have survived. This creative quest can be particularly admired when multiple impressions of the same plate are shown together, such as in the case of *The Descent from the Cross by Torchlight and Flight into Egypt: A Night Piece*. These spectacular nocturnal scenes confirm Rembrandt's reputation as the incontestable master of light and dark. *Rembrandt: Lightening the Darkness* guides the visitor through the artist's best known graphic masterpieces exploring his ingenious use of light and shade. At the beginning of the exhibition, you come face to face with the master himself in his self-portraits. They reveal a clear evolution in the artist's artistic and personal development, promoting himself as the Dutch Republic's greatest portraitist and printmaker. Later sections highlight his portraits – intimate family portrayals as well as commissioned ones – as well as episodes of the life and death of Jesus Christ, landscapes, scenes of daily life, and finally nude studies.

The first exhibition devoted to Rembrandt in Norfolk since 1990, this showing has been long overdue and will undoubtedly capture new audiences in Norfolk and beyond.

An Van Camp
Christopher Brown Curator of
Northern European Art
Ashmolean Museum of Art and
Archaeology, University of Oxford

Rembrandt: Lightening the Darkness
Introduction

Norwich Castle Museum & Art Gallery is privileged to have in its collections a group of ninety-three prints and one drawing by Rembrandt Harmenszoon van Rijn (1606-1669), one of the most outstandingly important figures in European art. The prints were bequeathed in 1951 by Percy Moore Turner (1877-1950), an art dealer, collector and admirer of Norwich School paintings, who spent part of his life in Norwich and was involved with the Castle and the artistic life of the city from the 1920s. He felt strongly that art should be seen by the public which resulted in his generous bequest to Norwich. The drawing came to us in 1978, accepted by HM Government in lieu of tax and allocated to Norwich. Between them these gifts give us a wonderful collection of Rembrandt's spectacular works on paper.

Rembrandt's fame as a painter needs little introduction, but fewer people today are aware of his ground-breaking significance as a printmaker. By the early seventeenth century prints were popular, but more as a means of reproduction than as an art form. Prints played an invaluable role in enabling the dissemination of artworks, more widely than had ever been possible before, but Rembrandt made the print a true work of art in its own right. Although he principally earned his living from painting, etching was not a subsidiary activity; he produced around 290 etchings throughout his life and is widely considered to be the most accomplished etcher of all time. His early fame across Europe was as a printmaker rather than a painter, achieving results in monochrome as expressive and varied as in his full palette of painted colours.

Rembrandt made his first etchings around 1626. He generally drew his subject straight onto the ground rather than basing it on preparatory drawings, and is known to have used a hydrochloric acid solution which 'worked slowly and did not make thin lines coarser.' (Eva Ornstein-Van Slooten and Marijke Holtrop, *The Rembrandt House: a catalogue of Rembrandt etchings*, Zwolle: WBOOKS; Amsterdam: Museum Het Rembrandthuis, 2016, p.12) Although a number of Rembrandt's prints are so-called 'only states', he often reworked his plates many times, creating different versions of the same print. His alterations could be minimal or extensive, and it is thought that no other artist in history reworked their plates as frequently as Rembrandt. Even during his lifetime, collectors sought out different states of the same etchings, which were often printed on diverse supports, including standard European paper, expensive Japanese and Chinese papers, a cheap wrapping paper known as cartridge or oatmeal paper, and vellum.

Rembrandt could achieve exceptional effects of light and dark as easily with a few sketchy lines as with detailed cross-hatching and drypoint etching. At least seventy-four of Rembrandt's plates are thought to have been sold after his bankruptcy in 1656. Prints were taken from these as late as 1916, so many posthumous impressions exist today.

Although created to accompany the exhibition *Rembrandt: Lightening the Darkness*, 21 October 2017 – 7 January 2018, this publication is nonetheless a standalone work. It introduces Rembrandt through the Norwich collection. We have selected a group of works which illustrate his most important subjects: portraiture and self-portraiture, the family, everyday life, religious subjects, landscapes and the nude. To all these subjects Rembrandt brought his unique blend of close observation, compassion and empathy. Through the use of black and white, light and shade, Rembrandt achieved a depth of expression in print which has perhaps never been equalled.

Francesca Vanke
Keeper of Art and Senior Curator of Decorative Art

Giorgia Bottinelli
Curator of Art

Norwich Castle Museum & Art Gallery,
Norfolk Museums Service

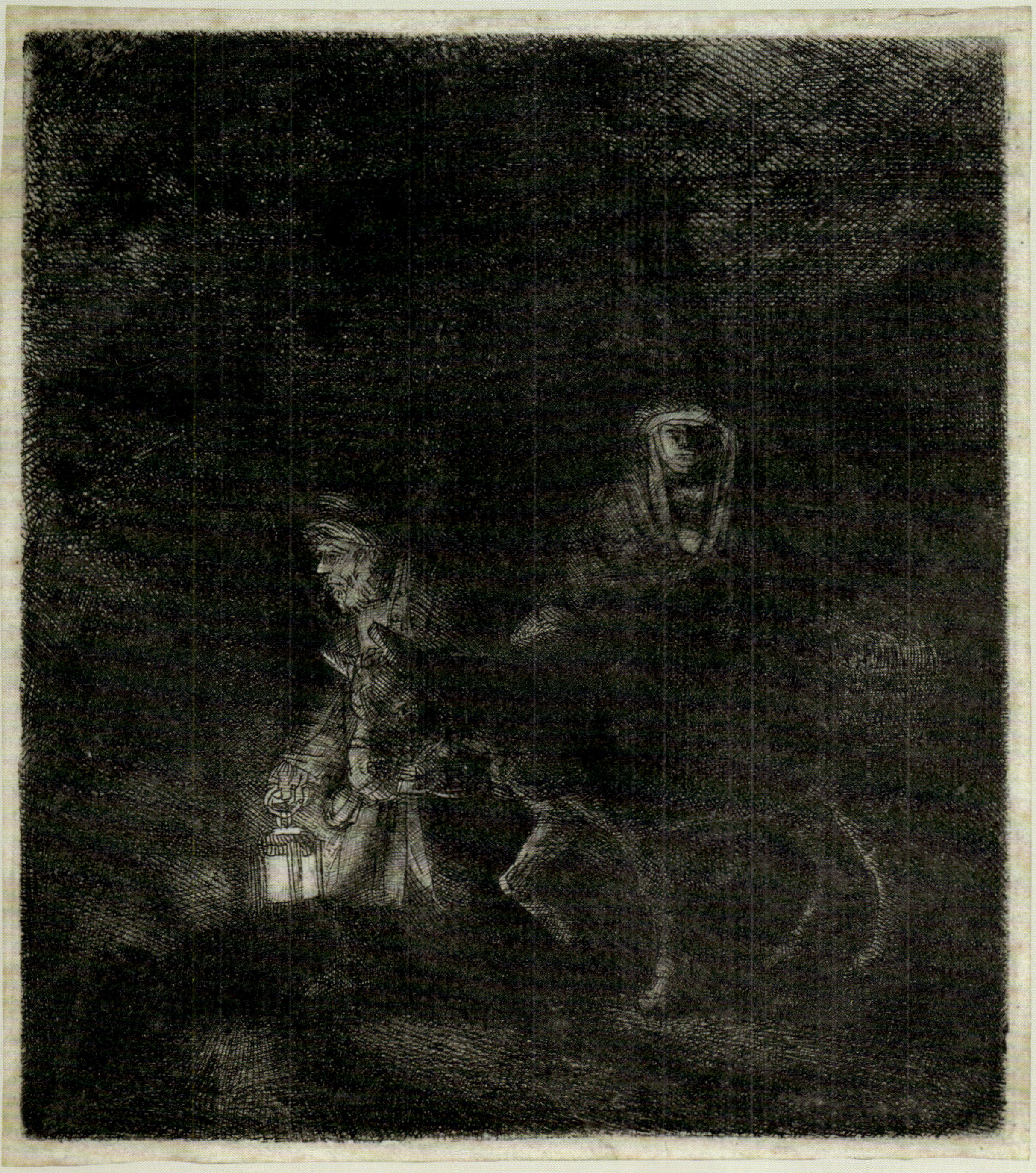

The Flight into Egypt: a night Piece (VI/X), 1651
Etching and drypoint on paper
12.6 x 11 cm
Signed and dated in plate lower right of subject 'Rembrandt f. 1651'
NWHCM : 1951.47.59

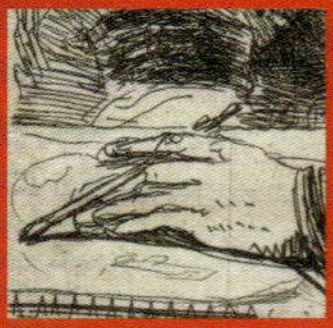

Rembrandt: Light and shadow

Rembrandt produced more self-portraits than almost any other artist. He is famed for the self-portraits he made throughout his life and documented his poignant journey from a fresh-faced youth, to a confident artist at the height of his power, to the sombre sixty-three year-old who had witnessed the death of his wife, his long-term lover and four of his five children, as well as fame, riches and bankruptcy. Within this large output is a series of thirty-two etched self-portraits, the great majority of which were made before 1640. The earliest of these were produced between 1628 and 1630 when he still lived in Leiden, his birthplace. Rembrandt used them to explore different facial expressions and the ways in which light from various directions fell on his face, highlighting and obscuring different elements each time. Depictions of often exaggerated facial expressions, known as 'tronies' ('heads'), were common in the Dutch Golden Age.

Rembrandt's self-portraits allow us to see him with different expressions, wearing a variety of costumes and, in one print, paired with his wife Saskia. Some seemingly sketchy and informal, others more posed, they exhibit similar characteristics in their expressiveness, their immediacy and humanity, all achieved purely through the means of monochrome print and the extraordinarily skilful use of light and shade. Rembrandt's lasting importance as an artist, and his genius, lie in a combination of qualities including an unparalleled talent for drawing, a rich awareness of colour, but also an almost uncanny ability to make simple black and white convey the essence of a person or a narrative. Rembrandt could capture mood and emotion in nothing more than a few black lines and the white space around them.

Self-portrait with Saskia, Busts (II/IV), 1636
Etching on paper
10.4 x 9.6 cm
Signed and dated in plate upper left of subject 'Rembrandt. f. / 1636'
NWHCM : 1951.47.17

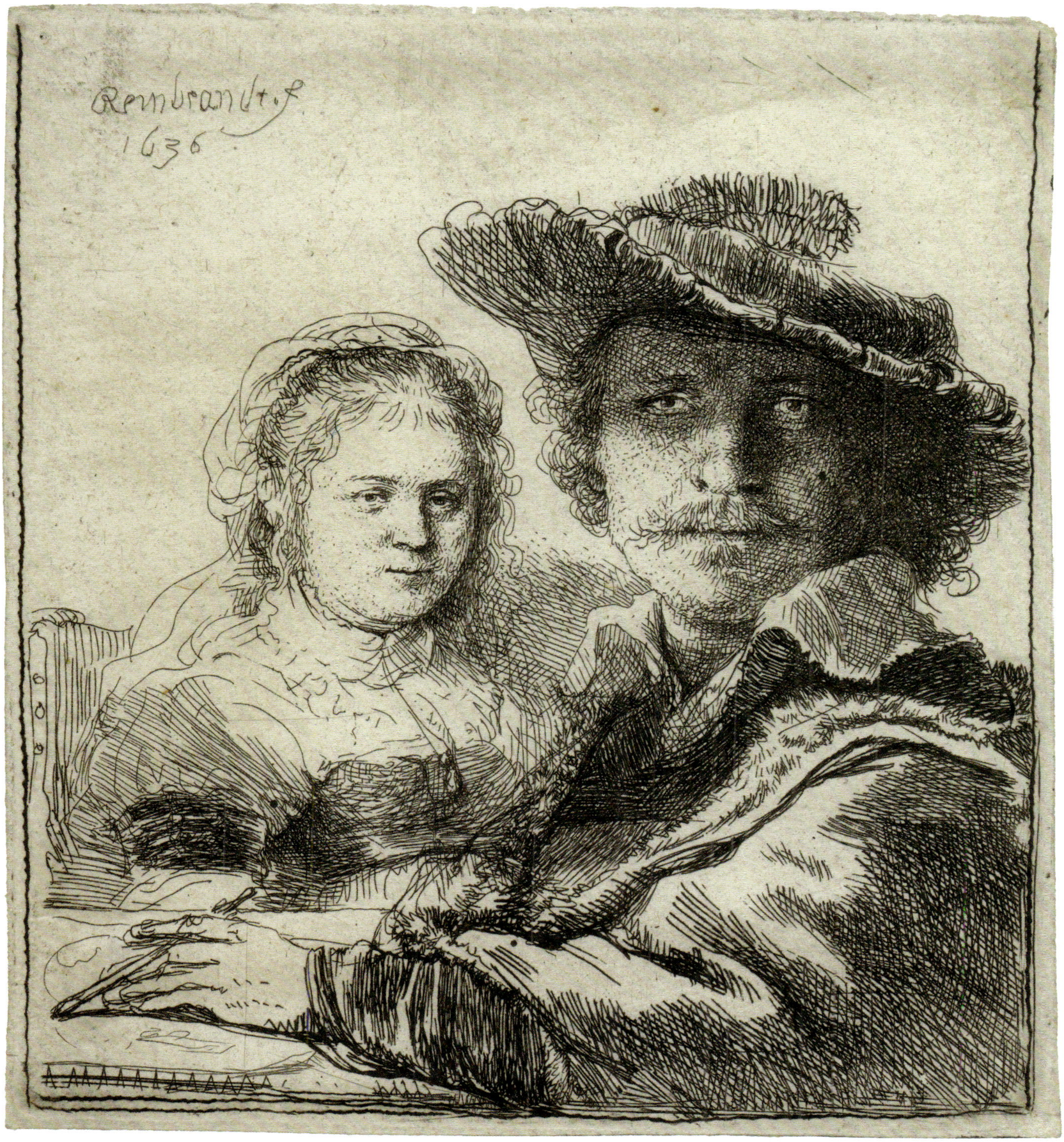
Rembrandt. f
1636

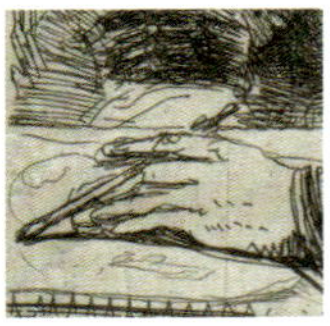

Self-portrait in a heavy Fur Cap, Bust (only state), 1631
Etching on paper
6.3 x 5.8 cm
Signed and dated in plate upper left of subject 'RHL 1631'
NWHCM : 1951.47.4

Rembrandt etched this self-portrait in 1631, when he was twenty-five years old. It was around this time that he moved from Leiden to Amsterdam, lodging in the house of the influential art dealer Hendrick van Uylenburgh on Sint Antoniesbreestraat, a broad street popular with artists and immigrants. The section where van Uylenburgh lived became known as Jodenbreestraat in the second half of the seventeenth century due to the influx of Jewish immigrants from Spain and Portugal.

By 1631 Rembrandt was already an established artist. Here he depicts himself as youthful but serious, wearing a fur cap and a coat with a contrasting fur-trimmed neck which might be signifiers of his status as an up-and-coming artist. Slanting light illuminates the right side of his face and throws the left into shadow, with the exception of his eye, which is picked out by the light and contributes to the intensity of his gaze. It is thought that Rembrandt originally conceived this portrait without the hat, as his curls and the top of his head are visible under it.

The portrait is signed 'RHL', which stands for 'Rembrandus Hermanni Leidenses' ('Rembrandt, son of Harmen, from Leiden'). He used this monogram until about 1632, continuing to identify himself as coming from Leiden for a while after moving to Amsterdam.

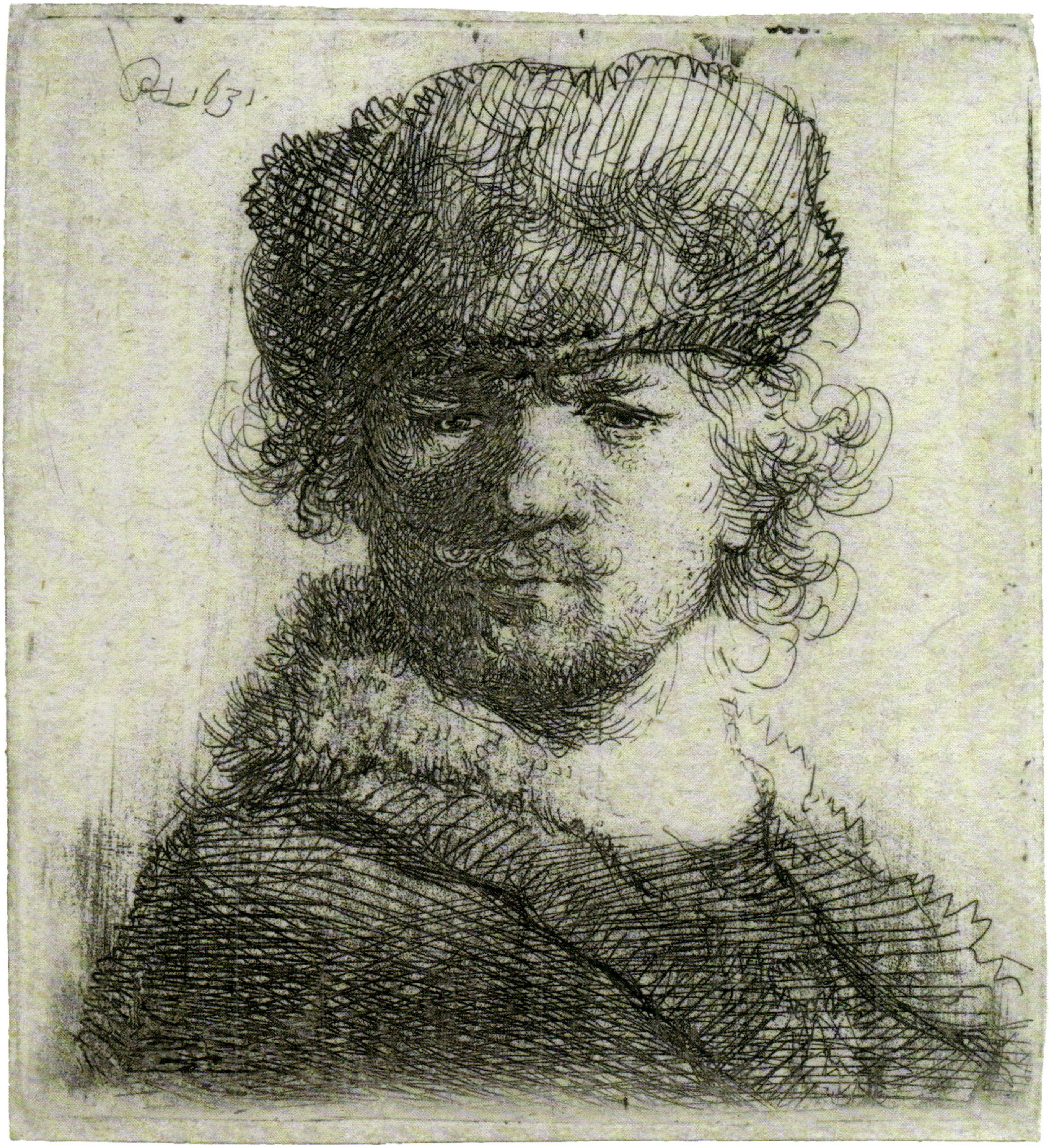
RL 1631

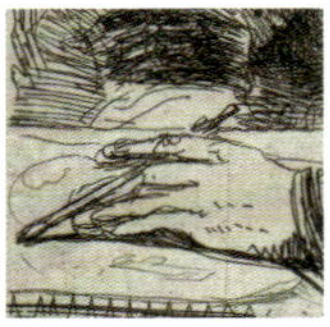

Self-portrait Wearing a soft Cap, full Face, Head only ('Rembrandt aux trois moustaches') (only state), 1634
Etching on paper
4.8 x 4.4 cm
NWHCM : 1951.47.11

Not much bigger than a modern passport photograph, this little etching depicts a very serene-looking Rembrandt. His face and cap are strongly illuminated from the right, throwing a shadow over his left shoulder; soft unruly curls tumble over one shoulder creating a sense of asymmetry in an otherwise frontal portrait. Although Rembrandt rendered his face and cap in great detail, he only used a few sketchy lines to hint at his collar in a shorthand manner. There is a quiet air of serenity and contentment about this etching which is absent from his more ostentatious, bombastic self-portraits.

On 22 June 1634 Rembrandt married Saskia van Uylenburgh, the niece of his art dealer Hendrick van Uylenburgh. Born in August 1612, she was six years younger than Rembrandt and came from a wealthy family in Leeuwarden in Friesland, where her father was mayor and a government attorney. Curiously, although it was Saskia who had married beneath her social status, it was her family, and not Rembrandt's, who attended their wedding. Between 1635 and 1640 Saskia gave birth to two girls and a boy who all died in infancy. Finally, in 1641 she gave birth to another boy, Titus, the only child who survived into adulthood.

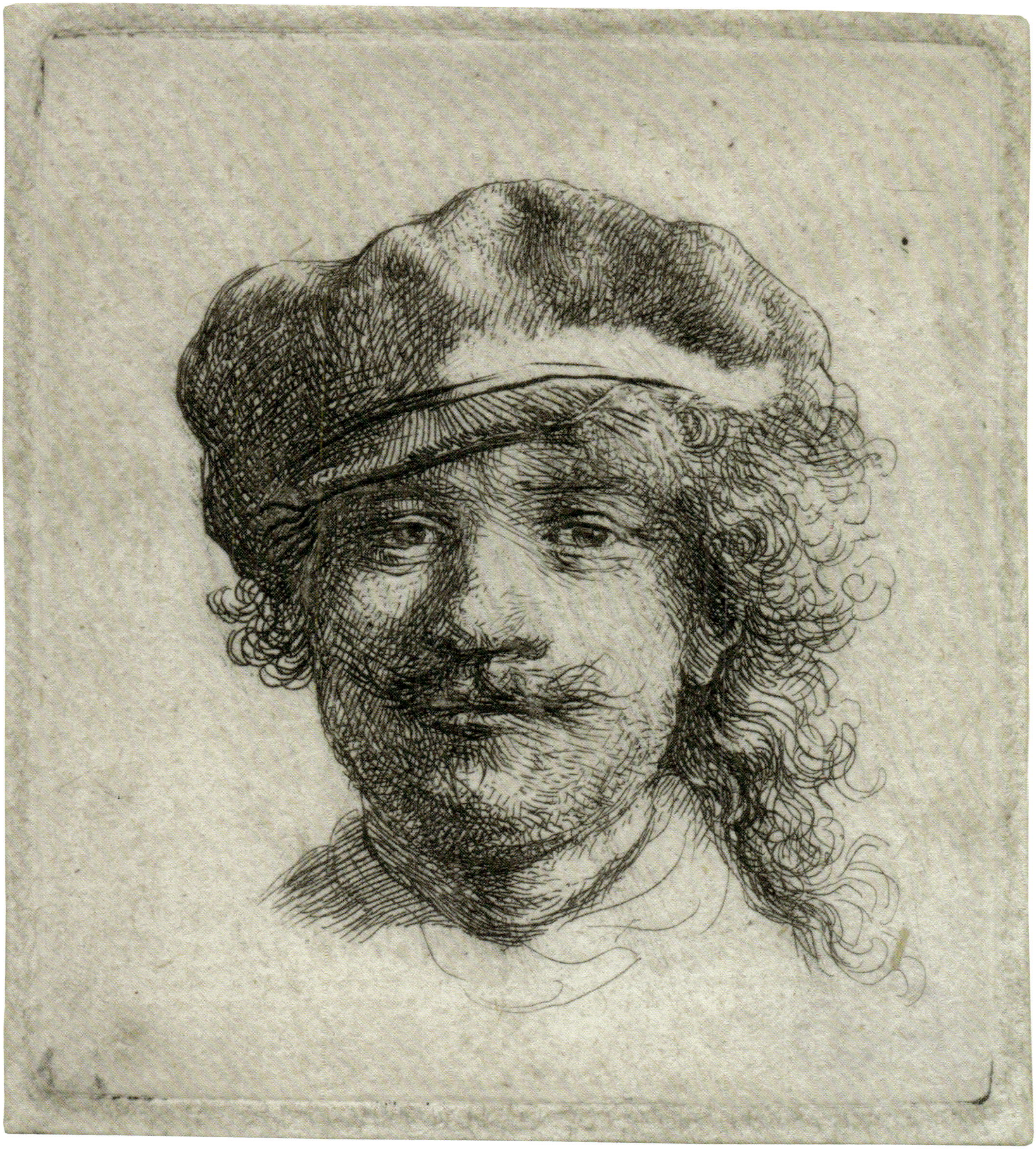

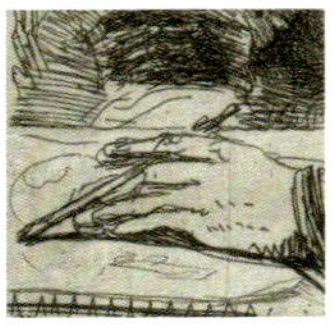

Self-portrait with raised Sabre (II/II), 1634
Etching with touches of burin on paper
12.4 x 10.2 cm
Signed and dated in plate upper left 'Rembrandt f. / 1634'
NWHCM : 1951.47.8

Dating from 1634, when Rembrandt was twenty-eight, this is a confident, haughty portrait; it is very different from the *Self-portrait Wearing a Soft Cap* of the same year. Here the artist has portrayed himself slightly frowning and holding a curved sabre or falchion-type weapon in a gloved hand; he is richly attired in an exotic costume with an ermine fur collar, embroidery and ruched cuffs, and wearing a cap topped with an ostrich feather, itself a signifier of luxury at the time as an expensive import from Africa.

Rembrandt has skilfully rendered the different textures of skin, hair, cloth, feather, leather and metal by altering his strokes, which are closer and more structured in the hat and body area, shorter and sparser to indicate fur, or loose arabesques to hint at embroidery.

In spite of the small dimensions of the print, which is smaller than a present-day postcard, there is something of the grand swagger portrait about it. Rembrandt cropped the image, making the subject appear closer to the front of the print and the viewer, and strengthening its confrontational feel.

Rembrandt owned a vast collection of costumes, armour, weapons and musical instruments which he utilised as props in his work. The inventory of his possessions, drawn up on 25 and 26 July 1656 following his bankruptcy, lists antique textiles, 'brightly coloured jackets', 'Indian costumes', antique helmets, breast plates and shields, and a large number of weapons including bows, crossbows, arrows and spears.

This is the second of two states of the print. Rembrandt's changes between the first and second state were minimal, consisting mostly of a slight reduction in the size of the plate.

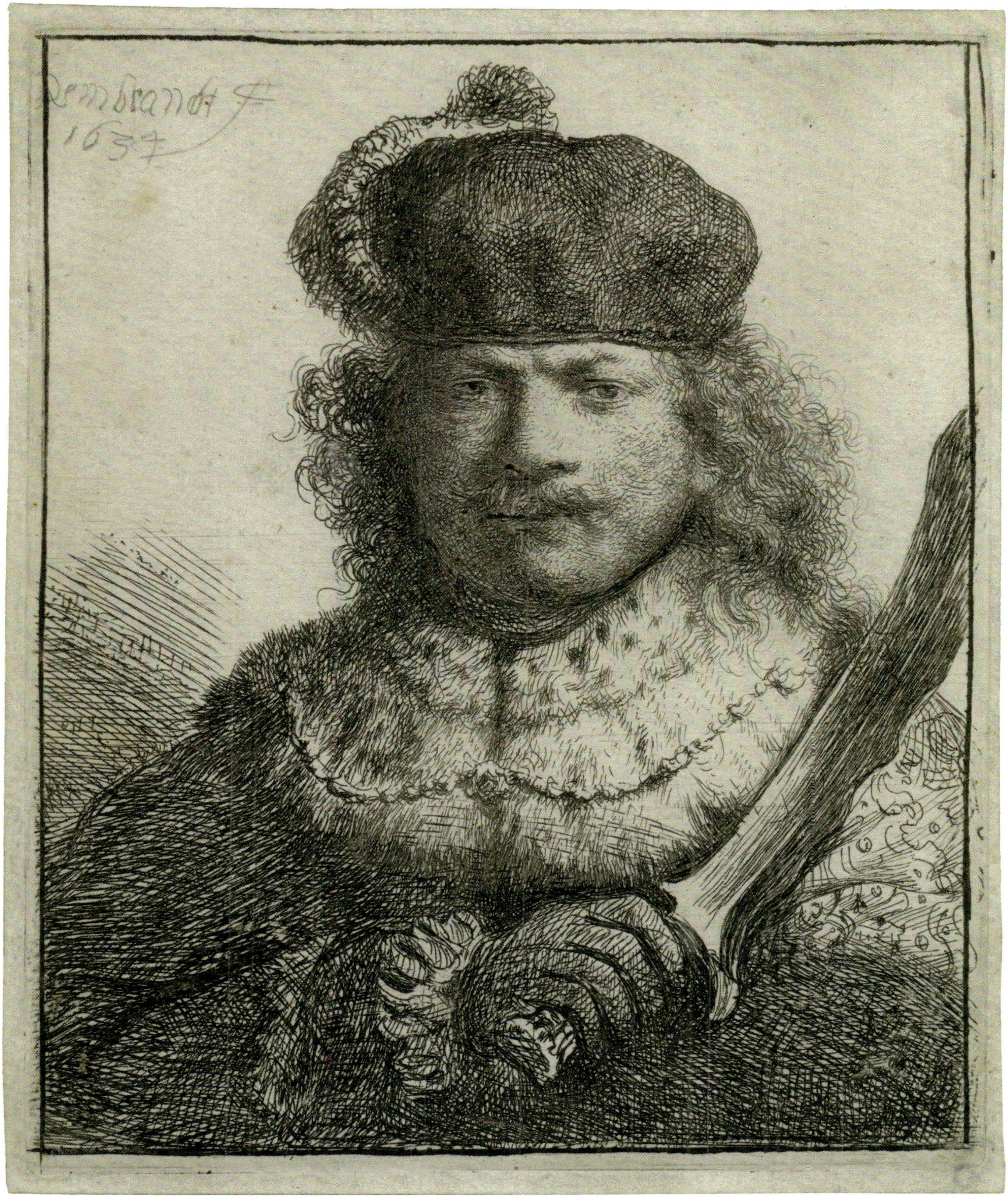
Rembrandt f
1634

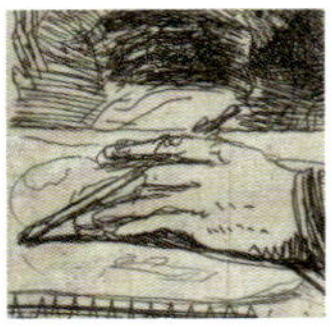

Self-portrait Leaning on a Stone-sill (II/II), 1639
Etching with touches of drypoint on paper
20.5 x 16.4 cm
Signed and dated in plate upper left 'Rembrandt f. / 1639'
NWHCM : 1951.47.27

Here Rembrandt has depicted himself in the guise of a nobleman. This print has been described as 'perhaps his most ambitious etched self-portrait' (Holm Bevers, Peter Schatborn and Barbara Welzel, *Rembrandt: the Master and his Workshop: Drawings and Etchings*, New Haven and London: Yale University Press; London: National Gallery Publications, 1991, p.200). With this etching and a painted self-portrait from 1640 (National Gallery, London), Rembrandt was drawing clear parallels between himself and Old Master painters. Indeed, both self-portraits borrow heavily from two Italian Renaissance portraits. Rembrandt's pose, with his body in profile, his face turned towards the viewer and his arm resting on a ledge, as well as the way the light hits the side of the face closer to the viewer, are directly inspired by Titian's *Portrait of Gerolamo (?) Barbarigo*, c.1510 (National Gallery, London), which in Rembrandt's time was thought to be a portrait of Ludovico Ariosto, the author of *Orlando Furioso*. The other great influence is Raphael's *Portrait of Baldassare Castiglione*, c.1514-15 (Musée du Louvre, Paris). Rembrandt's cap and ornate Renaissance costume with fur detailing are similar to Castiglione's, as is the rich, warm tonality of the painted self-portrait.

Curiously, in the late 1630s both of these Renaissance masterpieces were in the Netherlands. The Raphael painting was in Amsterdam before it was taken to Paris by the art dealer Alfonso Lopez, who worked for Cardinal Richelieu. The Titian had belonged to a Dutch merchant called Lucas van Uffelen, who had lived in Venice from 1615 and in the 1630s had returned to Amsterdam, where he died in 1638. In April 1639, a hugely important auction of van Uffelen's collection was held in the city. Rembrandt attended the sale and made an ink sketch of the Raphael (Albertina, Vienna), noting that it had been sold for 3,500 guilders. The purchaser was Alfonso Lopez, who subsequently took the painting to France.

The ledge at the front of the image creates the illusion of a space within the space. However, Rembrandt's voluminous sleeve overhanging the ledge, also borrowed from the Titian, breaks through this imaginary barrier and into the viewer's space. Although not a Catholic, Rembrandt curiously depicts himself wearing a crucifix, a small inclusion perhaps to strengthen the link he is creating between himself and the Italian Old Masters. At the time of his bankruptcy in 1656, Rembrandt owned two paintings by Raphael, four books of prints by or after Raphael and a book of Titian prints.

In the nineteenth century, our etching belonged to Friedrich August II, King of Saxony, an avid collector who owned 110,000 prints. His collector's stamp can be seen in the lower right corner.

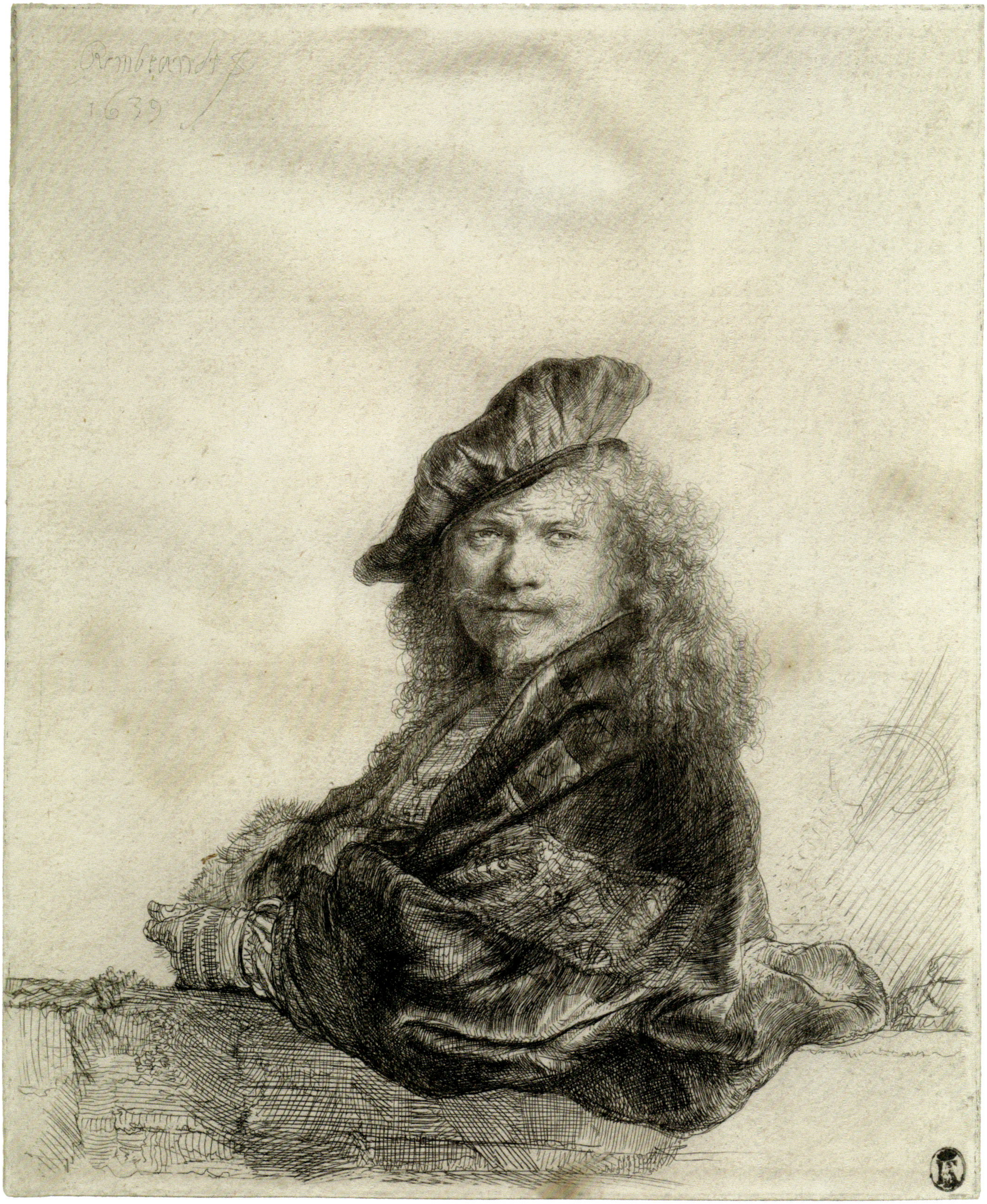
Rembrandt f
1639

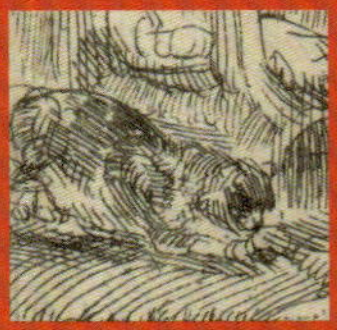

Illuminating the family

The story of Rembrandt's family life is well known. His marriage to Saskia van Uylenburgh was happy but short, as she died on 14 June 1642, before her thirtieth birthday. They had four children but three of them died in infancy. The only child who lived to adulthood was Titus, who was born in 1641 and died a year before his father. Rembrandt had two subsequent relationships, first with Titus' wet nurse Geertje Dircx and later with his housekeeper Hendrickje Stoffels.

Rembrandt's relationships were intense and in many cases tragically curtailed, and the family was an important subject in his art. In numerous works he portrayed family groups, old people, children and pets. He regularly depicted his own family members, with his parents providing subjects early in his career and his wife Saskia portrayed again and again during the 1630s, up to her death in 1642.

Rembrandt's parents were often used as models to study different light effects and facial expressions, much like his early self-portraits. Saskia was portrayed in all sorts of different guises, from the grand – such as her impersonation of the classical goddess Flora in the 1635 portrait *Saskia van Uylenburgh in Arcadian Costume* (National Gallery, London) – to the touchingly personal renditions of her confinements during pregnancy or illness. After Saskia's death this role was taken on by Hendrickje Stoffels. His son Titus was also the subject of many portraits from childhood into adulthood.

Although he never 'prettified' his subjects, Rembrandt always depicted them sympathetically. All Rembrandt's families share a common thread of humanity. Whether they represent beggars from the streets of Amsterdam or the Holy Family, they are all observed with meticulous attention to detail, and never without affection and insight. They are given 'real' faces, expressions and gestures and placed in convincing surroundings, often wearing contemporary Dutch dress, rather than being shown as generic tropes. Rembrandt always depicted them as worthy of the same level of attention and compassion, which makes all his subjects feel quintessentially human.

Peasant Family on the Tramp (II/III), 1652
Etching on paper
11 x 9.2 cm
NWHCM : 1951.47.69

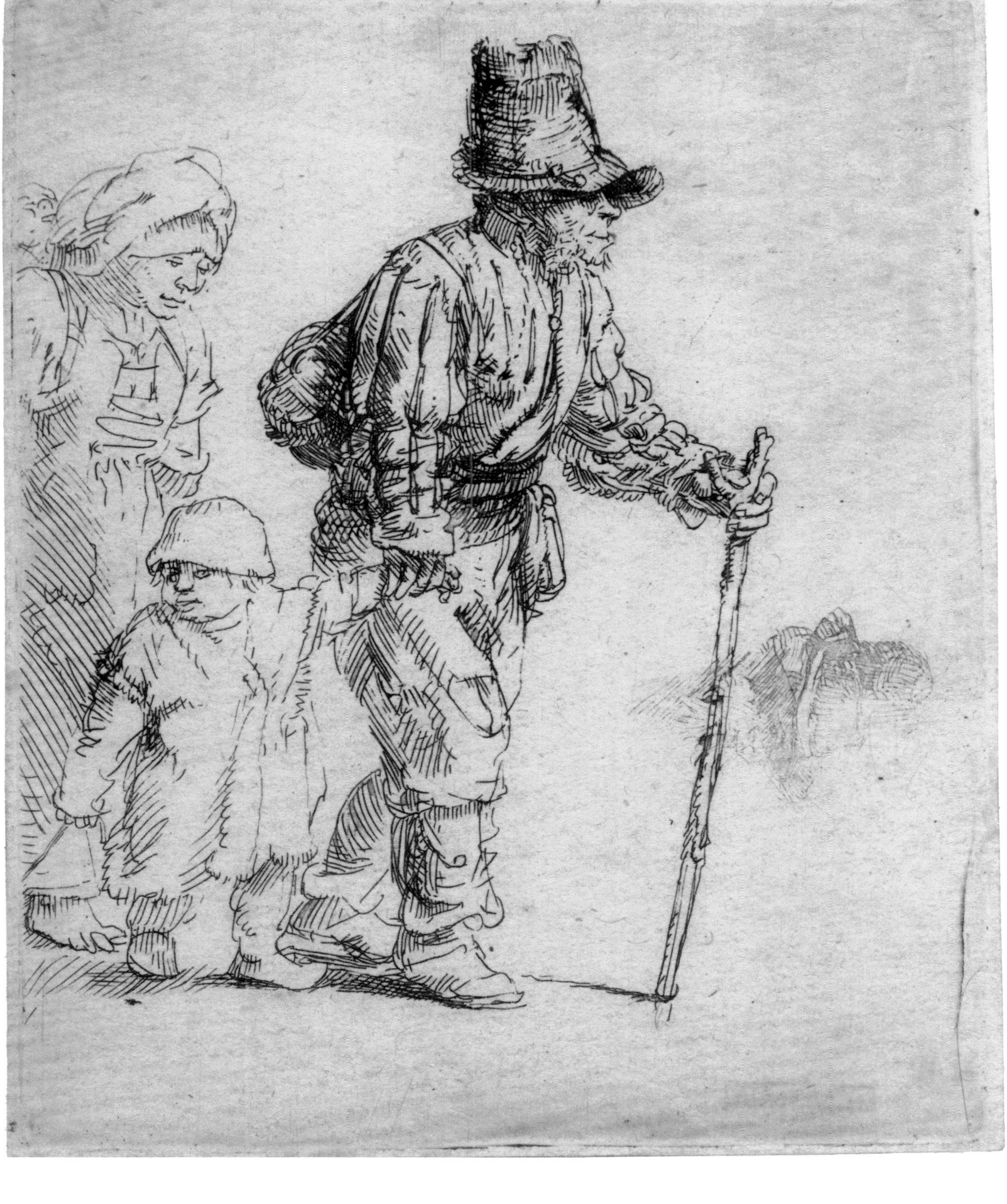

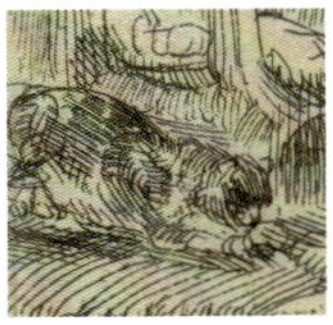

The Artist's Mother Seated at a Table, Looking right, three-quarter Length (II/III), 1631
Etching on paper
14.9 x 13.1 cm
Signed in plate lower centre left edge monogram 'RHL. f.'
NWHCM : 1951.47.6

Rembrandt's first dated etchings, from 1628, are small portraits of his mother. Cornelia Willemsdochter van Zuytbrouck (1568-1640), known as Neeltgen, married Harmen Gerritszoon van Rijn (c.1568-1630) in 1589. They had ten children, of whom Rembrandt was the ninth.

Rembrandt's father had died in April 1630 and here Rembrandt depicts his mother dressed in widow's garb. She is wearing a black veil over a tight-fitting coif, a black fur-trimmed cape over a black jacket and coat, and a white shirt which is simply indicated by a collar and cuffs. In front of her is a small table covered with a cloth. The table was not part of Rembrandt's initial composition and the diagonal line of his mother's skirt can be seen underneath, continuing below her knee towards the lower right corner of the composition.

With the exception of an area behind the sitter, where shadow is depicted in loose cross-hatched lines, Rembrandt has left the background completely blank to focus the attention on the main figure. Indeed, in a bold move, he left half of the paper deliberately unmarked.

Neeltgen is shown sitting in an armchair, hands clasped, looking out to the right of the picture. She appears to be lost in contemplation. Light coming from the right picks out details from Neeltgen's chair such as the back and armrest. It rests on her venerable face criss-crossed by lines, on her pursed lips and on her hands, emphasising her raised veins. It also highlights the different textures of her all-black clothing. All is still, quiet and contemplative. The expanse of white space helps to achieve this impression of serenity.

Already during Rembrandt's lifetime this impression is thought to have belonged to Pierre Mariette II (1634-1716) in Paris. Mariette was an influential art dealer and publisher, as well as a great print collector. His signature is often found on the reverse of prints from his collection; the earliest found is on a Rembrandt etching and dated 1646, when Mariette was only twelve years old.

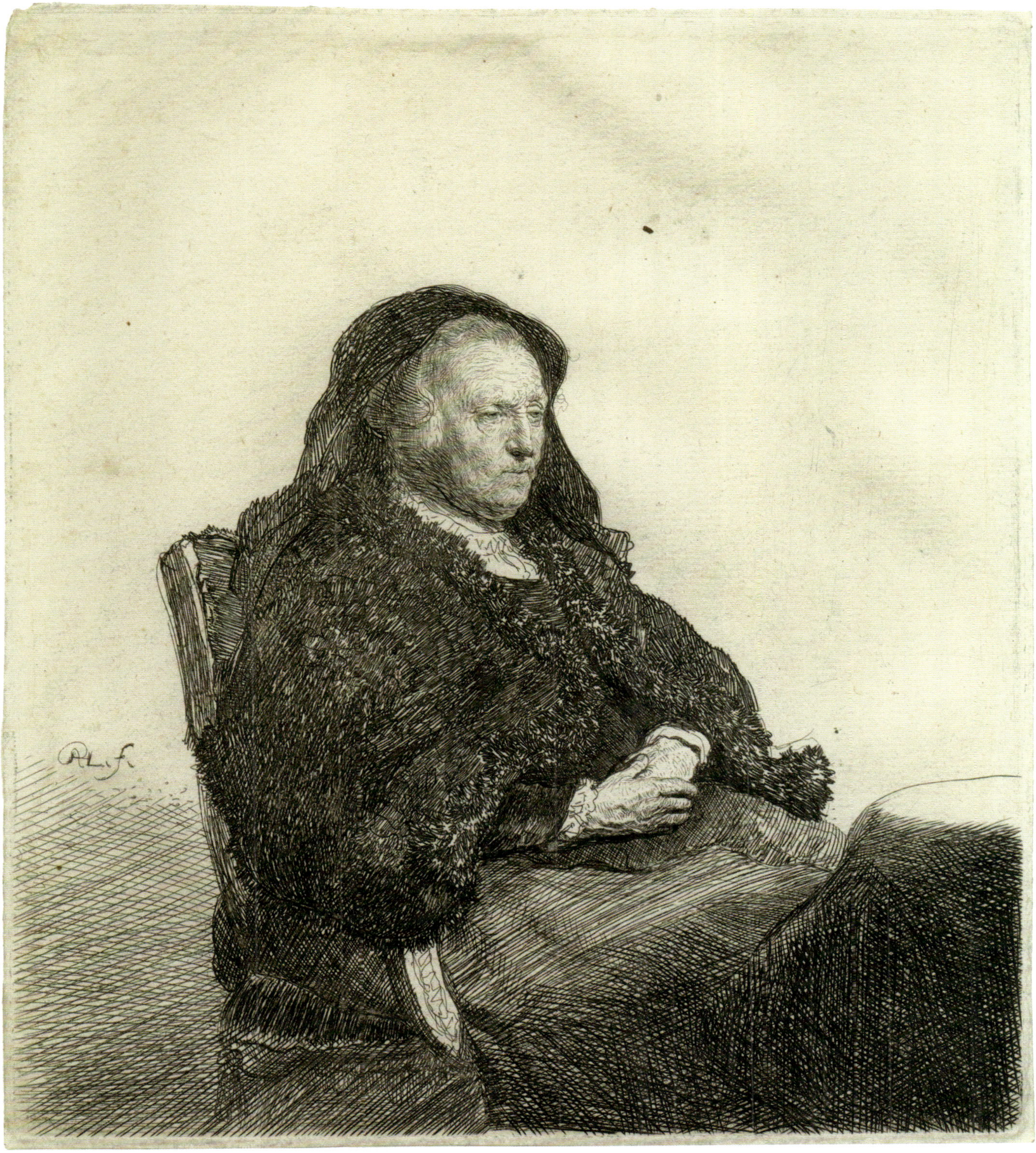

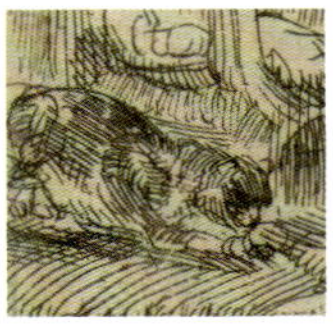

Abraham Caressing Isaac (I/IV), 1637
Etching on paper
11.6 x 8.9 cm
Signed in plate lower left of subject 'Rembrandt f.'
NWHCM : 1951.47.20

The Bible was Rembrandt's most important source of inspiration and biblical subjects account for the largest number of prints in his oeuvre. The story of Abraham and his family must have particularly appealed to Rembrandt as he turned to it again and again over a period of approximately twenty years. Norwich Castle owns four prints depicting different events in the life of Abraham, of which this is the earliest.

The figure of Abraham holds an important place in Christianity, Judaism and Islam. Born in a polytheistic society in Ur, Mesopotamia (modern-day Iraq), Abraham is married to his half-sister Sarah, who is ten years younger than him and infertile. In old age, Abraham has several visions telling him to leave Ur and settle in a land God would show him, where he would become the progenitor of new nations. In order to fulfil the prophecy that he would be the father of many, Sarah offers Abraham her servant Hagar, who gives birth to his son Ishmael when Abraham is eighty-six.

Thirteen years later, when he is ninety-nine, Abraham receives a visit from three angels who announce that Sarah would bear him a son the following year. Sarah laughs incredulously when she hears this and, when she gives birth to a son a year later, she names him Isaac, which means 'he will laugh'. As a result of Isaac's birth and with God's approval, Sarah convinces Abraham to send Hagar and Ishmael away. Soon after comes the most important test of Abraham's faith, when God asks him to sacrifice Isaac. As Abraham is about to strike Isaac with a sacrificial knife God, satisfied with Abraham's obedience, sends an angel to stop him.

Rembrandt depicted the sacrifice of Isaac in a number of dramatic paintings, drawings and etchings, but here he portrayed a more homely moment, with a young, laughing Isaac holding an orange and leaning on his aged father, who is stroking his face. Both father and son are dressed in sumptuous clothing, Abraham in a fur-trimmed cloak and Isaac in a long, tasselled coat. Commentators have identified this scene, which takes place outdoors, with the moment immediately preceding the removal of Hagar and Ishmael (Erik Hinterding, *Rembrandt Etchings from the Frits Lugt Collection*, vol.1, Bussum: THOTH Publishers; Paris: Fondation Custodia, 2008, p.75). This would account for the contrast between Isaac's carefree demeanour and Abraham's sombre appearance. The way Rembrandt has lit the scene draws attention to Abraham's eyes, staring gravely straight at the viewer.

Some art historians believe that the subject of this print is actually *Jacob Caressing Benjamin*, but the attribution appears less convincing than *Abraham Caressing Isaac*.

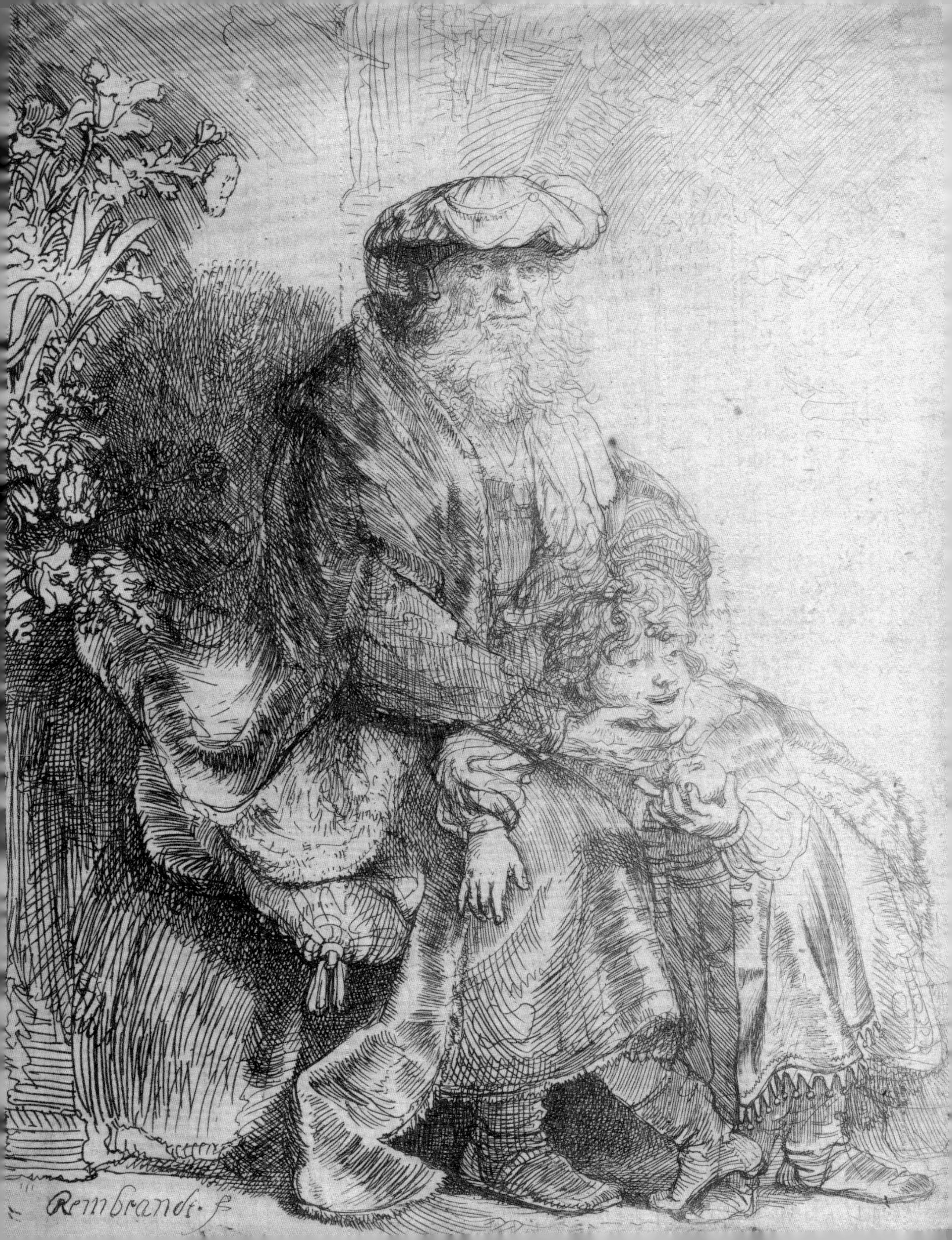
Rembrandt f

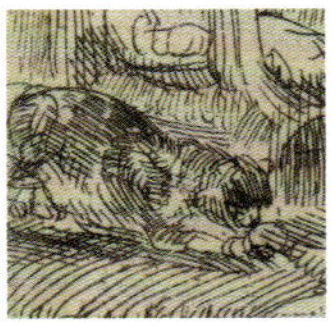

Sheet of Studies, with a Woman ill in Bed (only state), 1639
Etching on paper
13.8 x 15.2 cm
NWHCM : 1951.47.24

This is an unusual print. It shows a mixture of different subjects including two portraits of Saskia ill in bed, three old men, a beggar couple and a man's head. Some of the figures are detailed while others are roughly sketched, and two are depicted at a 90-degree angle from the other six. At first glance it looks like a series of quick drawings made in a sketchbook, something an artist would do 'on the spot', to explore different subjects or to work up a composition. However, it is a finished product which has gone through all the laborious stages of etching, such as grounding the plate, drawing on the ground, biting the plate, removing the ground and printing. Its spontaneous nature is partially due to the fact that Rembrandt usually drew straight onto the etching ground rather than relying on preparatory drawings.

Most of Rembrandt's etched sheets of studies were made between 1632 and 1638; many of them depicted Saskia, often more than once on the same sheet. There are also several drawings of Saskia, frequently in bed. The British Museum owns a sketch from 1635-40 (*A Woman Lying awake in Bed*) and Rotterdam's Museum Boijmans Van Beuningen has a particularly poignant pen-and-ink drawing, *Four Studies of Rembrandt's Wife Saskia*, with three sketches depicting her lying in bed and one holding their first-born son Rombertus, who had been named after Saskia's father and died at the age of two months.

The stamp visible in the lower right corner of the print refers to a previous owner of this print, Edward Vernon Utterson (1775/6-1856), a lawyer, fellow of the Society of Antiquaries and a great collector of books, prints and drawings. The print was then sold to John Malcolm, Laird of Poltalloch (1805-1893), who also owned our drawing *Group of Musicians Listening to a Flute Player* (see p.70-71). An eminent art connoisseur, Malcolm amassed a magnificent collection of around 1,400 Old Master prints and drawings, most of which was sold to the British Museum after his death.

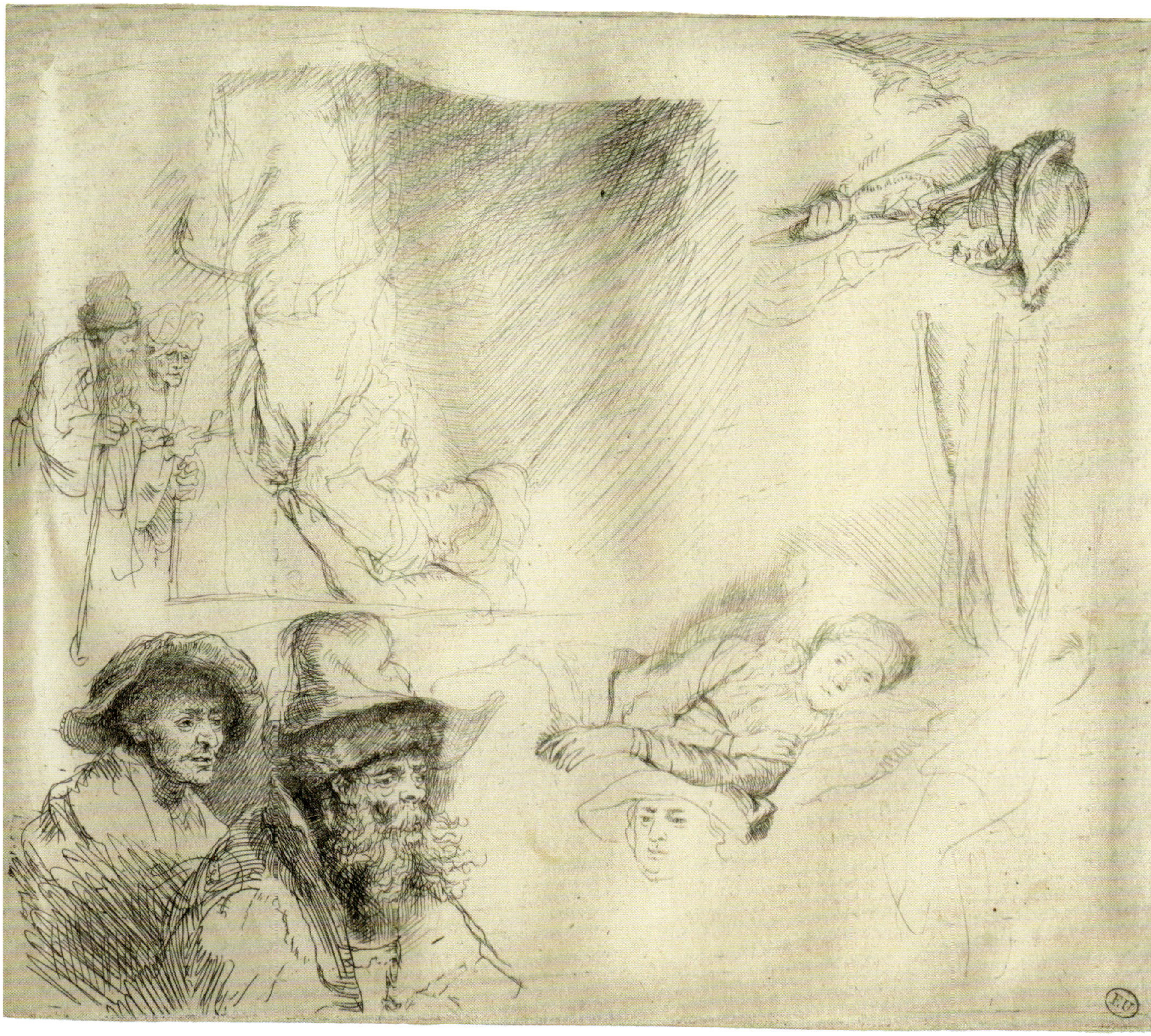

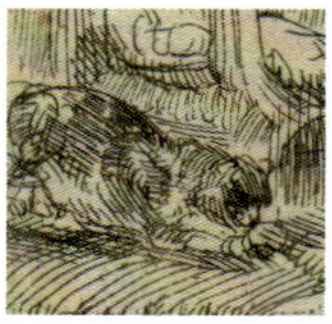

The Death of the Virgin (II/V), 1639
Etching and drypoint on paper
39.5 x 31 cm
Signed and dated in plate lower left of subject 'Rembrandt f. 1639'
NWHCM : 1951.47.25

In Rembrandt's time the Calvinist Church Council was the predominant religious authority in Amsterdam, but it appears that other Protestants, Catholics and Jews were tolerated in the city. Although likely, it is not known if Rembrandt was baptised as a Calvinist, but as an adult he was not a member of the Calvinist Church.

The Reformer John Calvin (1509–1564) had condemned religious images, including images of Mary, as idolatrous. He rejected the Catholic veneration of Mary as diminishing the importance of Jesus. The life of Mary, however, plays a huge part in Catholic iconography, so it would seem that Rembrandt made this etching specifically for a Catholic audience.

The death of the Virgin was a common subject in art. In Rembrandt's time it had been tackled most recently, not to mention controversially, by Caravaggio (1571-1610) in Rome in 1601-4. Although Rembrandt never travelled to Italy, his teacher Pieter Lastman (1583–1633) had worked in Rome between 1604 and 1607 and was strongly influenced by Caravaggio. However, the most direct influence on Rembrandt's composition was a 1510 woodcut of the same title by Albrecht Dürer (1471-1528), which he is known to have purchased at auction in 1638.

From Dürer's composition Rembrandt borrowed the heavy drapery over the bed, pulled back to reveal Mary, and Mary's position, slumped over thick pillows. His scene is more expansive than Dürer's, which appears to take place in a small, enclosed chamber. Rembrandt has also added a large crowd of mourners displaying a variety of sorrowful expressions. Among the onlookers is a woman drying her eyes, one clutching at a bedpost in despair, one kneeling with her hands clasped in prayer, a man leaning forward on the bed and another opening his arms in a gesture of anguish. Curiously, he also added two girls and a boy in the corner, who are turning away from the unfolding events. Some costumes give the scene a non-specific oriental feel.

Rembrandt has depicted Mary's suffering in a realistic manner by including a man adjusting her pillow to make her comfortable and a grave-looking doctor taking her pulse. These would have been regular activities in Rembrandt's home throughout Saskia's illnesses. At the same time, a group of angels and putti on a cloudbank breaks through the ceiling's architecture, adding a sense of supernatural drama and introducing a shaft of bright, divine light shining straight on Mary in her bed on a raised platform. In doing so Rembrandt shows the earthly and celestial effortlessly coexisting on the same plane.

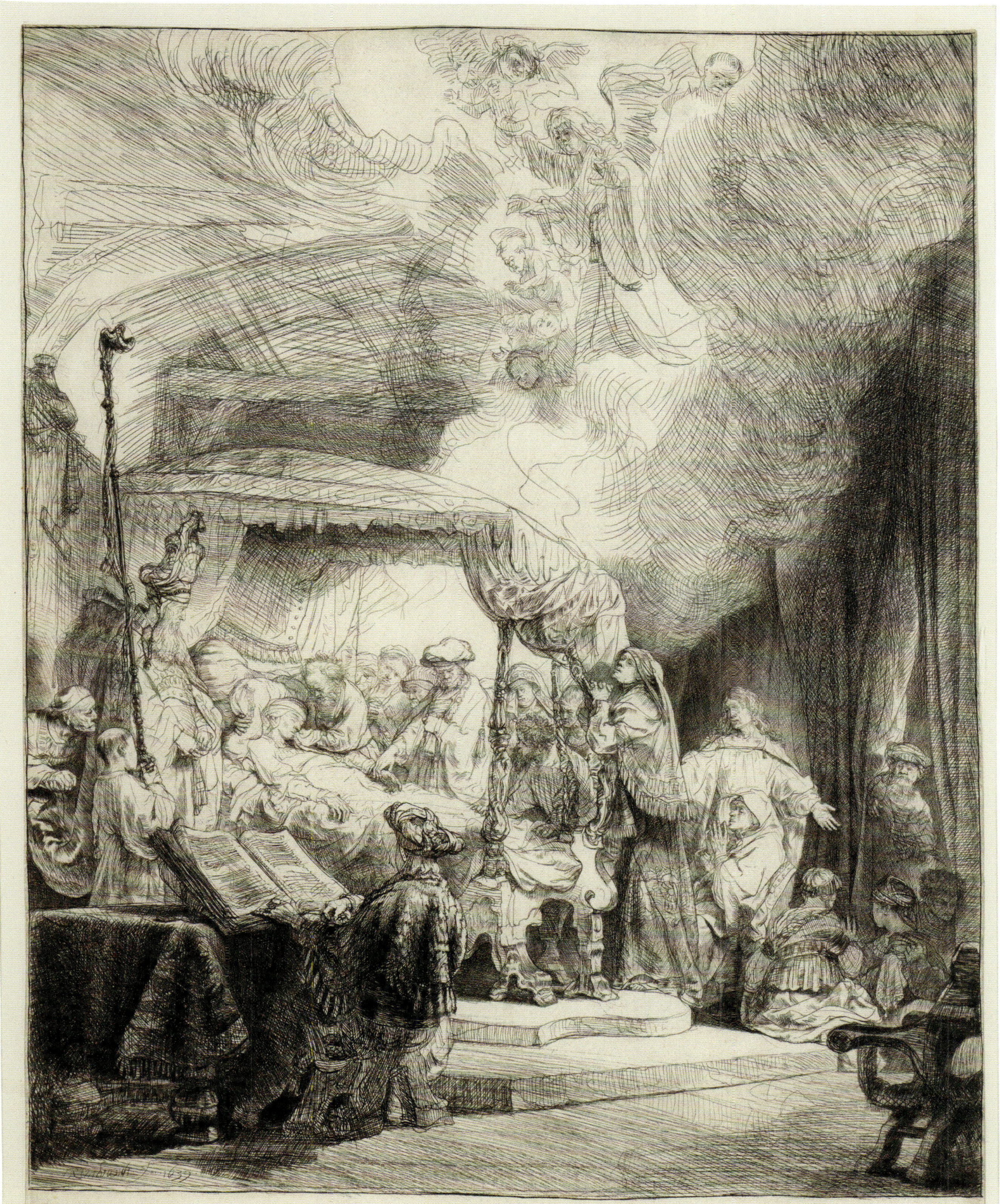

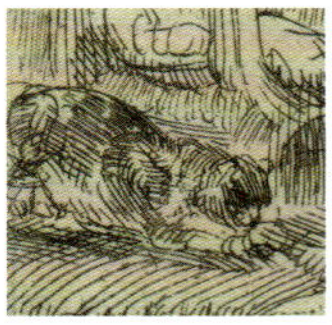

Death Appearing to a wedded Couple from an open Grave
(only state), 1639
Etching and drypoint on paper
10.9 x 7.8 cm
Signed and dated in plate lower left 'Rembrand [sic] f. 1639'
NWHCM : 1951.47.26

To modern eyes, this appears to be a somewhat macabre subject. However, death was much more part of daily life in the seventeenth century and the *memento mori*, or reminder of death, was a popular motif in art. The plague affected Amsterdam at least four times during Rembrandt's life (in 1623-5, 1635-6, 1655 and 1663-6) and mortality rates were high – over ten percent of the population with each outbreak. Rembrandt's lover Hendrickje Stoffels would die of the plague in 1663. Infant mortality was also high and affected Rembrandt's household as it did many others. By the time Rembrandt made this etching, he and Saskia had already lost two children: their son Rombertus, named after Saskia's father, had died aged two months in February 1636 and their daughter Cornelia, named after Rembrandt's mother, had died in August 1638, when she was only one month old. Their next daughter, also named Cornelia, would die before she reached one month in 1640.

This allegorical scene depicts Death in the shape of a skeleton, rising from a grave. Casually resting against his scythe, he proffers an hourglass to a young couple holding hands. The hourglass is a symbol of time unavoidably running out, and therefore of death. The well-dressed couple, wearing feathered hats and sumptuous costumes, does not seem to be perturbed by the apparition. Indeed, the young man is smiling down at Death while raising his left hand in greeting. The young woman, who is wearing a flat hat similar to the one Saskia wears in some portraits, appears to be offering him a flower, in itself a symbol of the transience of life.

Rembrandt made only one state of this print. It is lightly etched with some drypoint. Some parts are only barely sketched using quick, free lines. The young man's bust is much less defined than his face and legs; the foreground is minimal, with a handful of lines summarily indicating vegetation; a slight, just-indicated shape behind the grave may represent a framed mirror, an incongruous addition to a graveyard scene.

In the eighteenth century this print belonged to John Barnard (1709-1784), one of the foremost art collectors of his time. His collection of drawings and 12,000 prints was of the highest quality, and some of his Rembrandt prints are reputed to have come from the collection of Jan Six, Rembrandt's friend and patron.

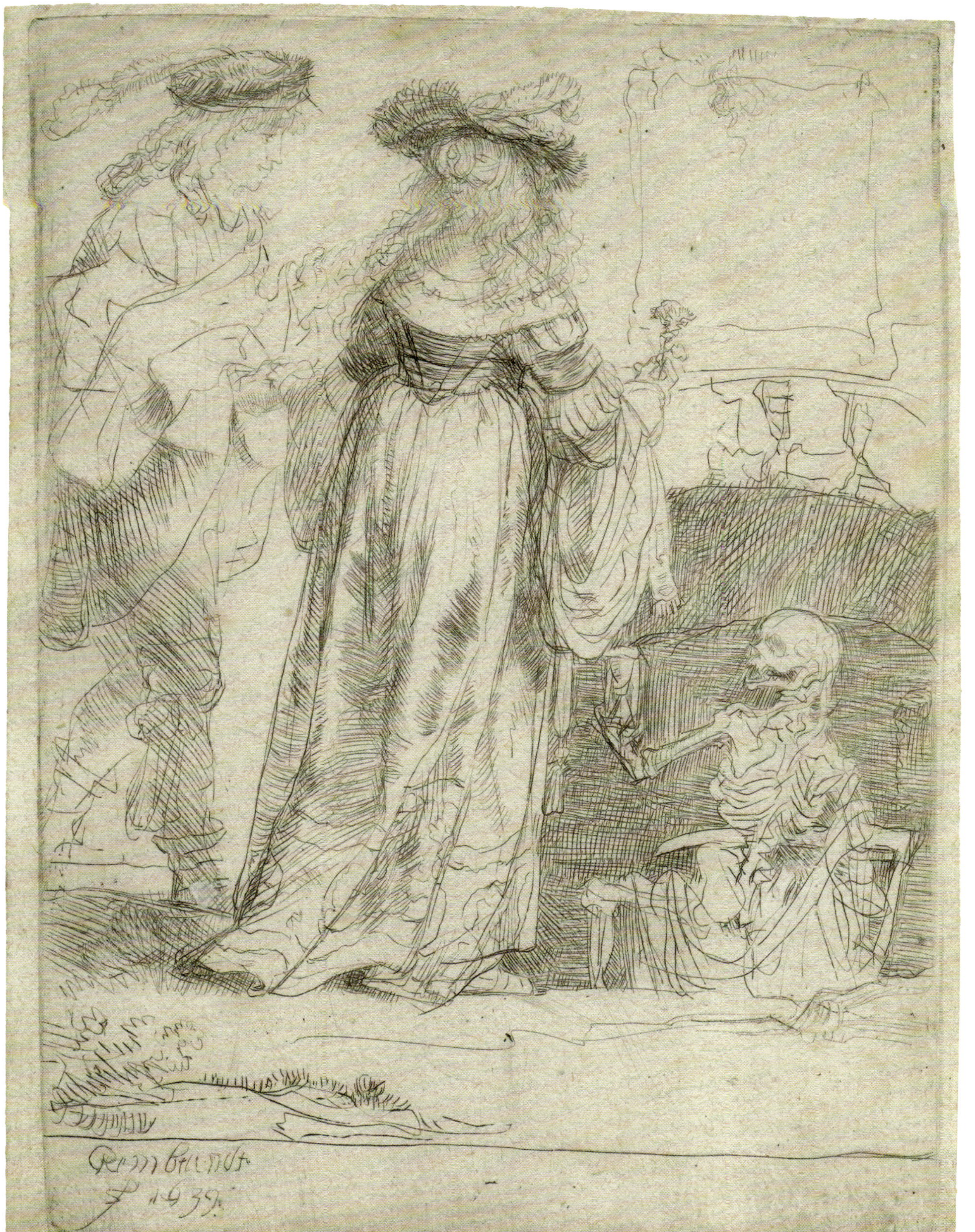
Rembrandt
f 1639

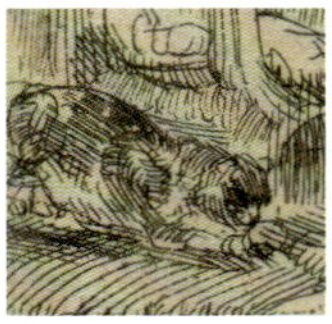

The Virgin and Child with the Cat and the Snake (I/IV), 1654
Etching on paper
9.5 x 14.4 cm
Signed and dated in plate lower centre of subject 'Rembrandt. f. 1654.'
NWHCM : 1951.47.75

In 1654 Rembrandt embarked on a small series of prints from the childhood of Christ. 1654 was also the year of the birth of Rembrandt and Hendrickje Stoffels' daughter. She was named Cornelia like Rembrandt's earlier daughters, who had died in infancy. It is tempting to draw comparisons between this event in Rembrandt's life and the way he depicted the relationship between Mary and the infant Jesus in this print.

Rembrandt has portrayed Mary and the baby Jesus in a domestic environment, with a fire in the foreground and an open trunk with fabric spilling out onto the floor. Mary is depicted wearing contemporary Dutch clothing, but the leaded window behind provides a convenient halo behind her head. Mary and Jesus are shown as completely self-absorbed and self-contained. The tight, almost spiralling unit comes directly from Andrea Mantegna's engraving *Madonna and Child*, 1470-80. Rembrandt owned a book of prints by Mantegna (1431-1506), described in the 1656 inventory as 'Mantegna's precious book', but it is not known whether this included a reproduction of his *Madonna and Child*. Rembrandt also included Joseph in the scene but placed him outside the room looking in, physically and psychologically separate from the mother-and-child unit. Unusually, the light comes into the room from the window at the back, backlighting the main protagonists, who are almost silhouetted against it with their faces in shadow.

In this print Mary is shown stepping on a snake. This is a common motif in Catholic iconography, with Mary seen as a second Eve who would conquer original sin. The throne to the left of the scene alludes to Mary's role as 'Queen of Heaven', but Rembrandt shows her sitting on the floor according to the less-known fourteenth-century Italian motif of the *Madonna dell'umiltà*, or 'Madonna of humility'. The fourteenth century was a time of great Papal wealth and power, but also witnessed the rise of the so-called 'poor orders', such as the Franciscans and Dominicans; the *Madonna dell'umiltà* served to remind viewers that Jesus – rather than material riches – was the greatest treasure in life.

On the left of the etching a cat is seen playing with the hem of Mary's robe. Although cats sometimes embody evil in Christian iconography, the association between cats and Mary is a positive one. Tradition has it that in the stable at Bethlehem a cat jumped into Jesus' crib while he was crying and fell asleep next to him, soothing him with its warmth. The 'M'-shaped markings on the foreheads of tabby cats are said to have originated when Mary patted the cat on the head in the stable, bestowing her mark upon it.

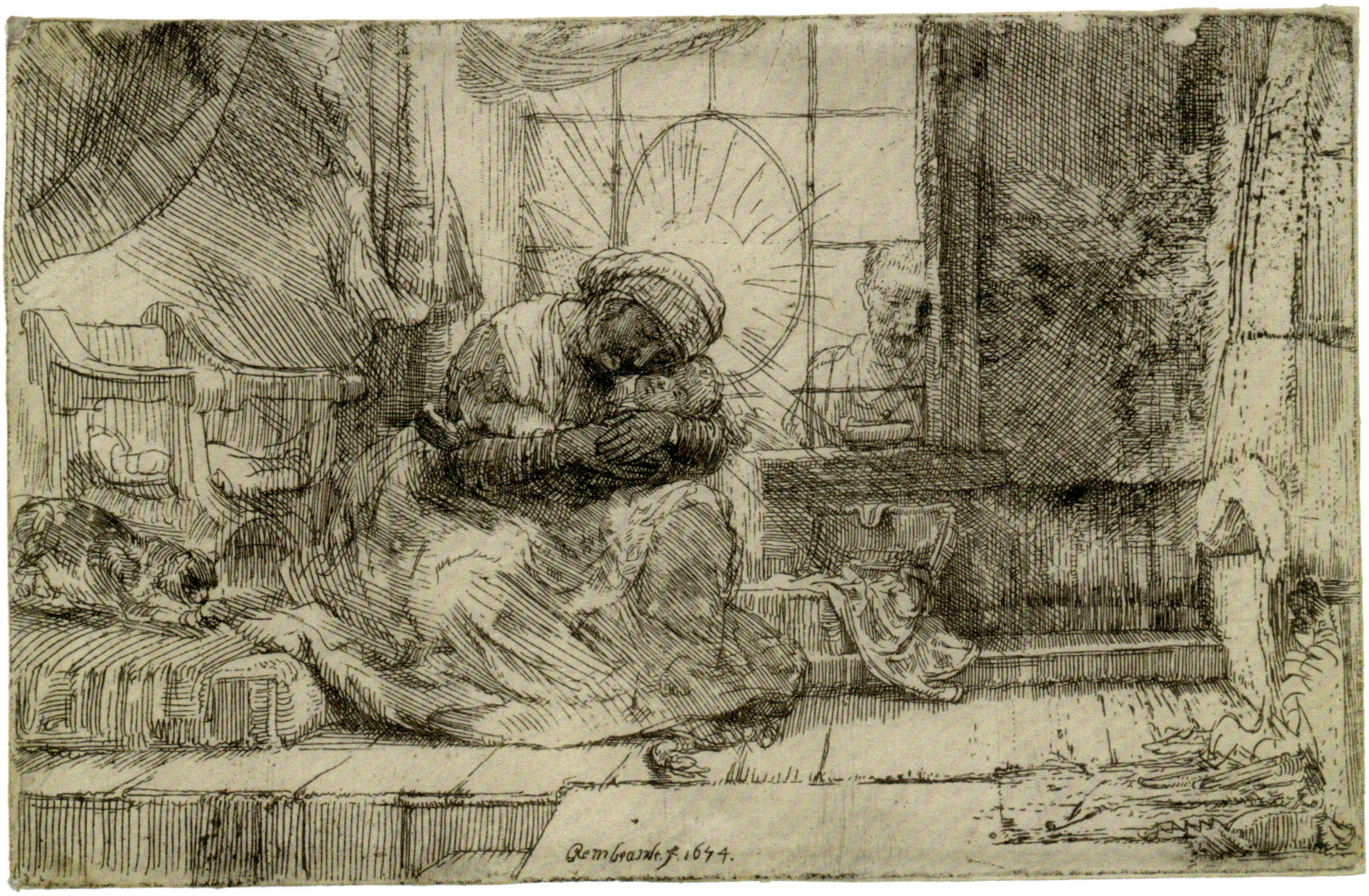
Rembrandt f. 1654

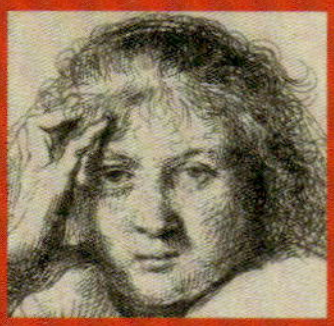

The light within

At the height of his career, Rembrandt was much in demand as an artist, and he portrayed some of the leading figures in Amsterdam society. His painted portraits remain some of the most famous in western art, now admired in museums worldwide. However, his skill at rendering light and shadow ensured that his portraits in the medium of print are similarly arresting and atmospheric, with an equal ability to illuminate a subject's individual character. Most of Rembrandt's patrons who commissioned portraits in print did so for personal circulation among friends and family. These portrait prints are now rarer than many of Rembrandt's other subjects because, once completed, the plates usually became the property of the sitters themselves, who would have only as many copies printed as they saw fit. Prints being cheaper to commission than painted portraits, Rembrandt's etched portraits include many middle class associates and acquaintances. Among these were a physician, a preacher, a print dealer and a goldsmith, as well as anonymous individuals in whom the artist was capturing the details of a mood or facial expression, qualities in which light and shadow play a vital part in bringing faces to life. The fineness and precision achievable through the etching or drypoint medium lends itself to portraying skin tone, hair and facial lines in exquisite detail. Monochrome black and white also focuses attention on the pared-down economy of Rembrandt's drawing: not a single line superfluous to the achievement of the end result.

Rembrandt revealed the personalities of his wide variety of sitters at all stages of life. He was known to love fine costumes and accessories. He included these in portraits of himself and others, but never allowed them to overshadow or distract from his renderings of character. In works such as *Old Man with Divided Fur Cap* the fine headdress indicates status, but it is counteracted by the old man's wrinkled face and clenched hand knotted with arthritis. Similarly, in *Three Heads of Women, one Lightly Etched*, depicting his wife Saskia in different poses, Rembrandt captures her attractive, warm expression, but does not idealise her. Her double chin is equally evident. In these as in all his printed portraits Rembrandt mingled his subjects' dignity with vulnerability, seeing clearly but without judgement.

Head of a Man in a Fur Cap, Crying out (IV/VI), 1629
Etching with touches of drypoint and burin on paper
3.4 x 2.8 cm
NWHCM : 1951.47.2

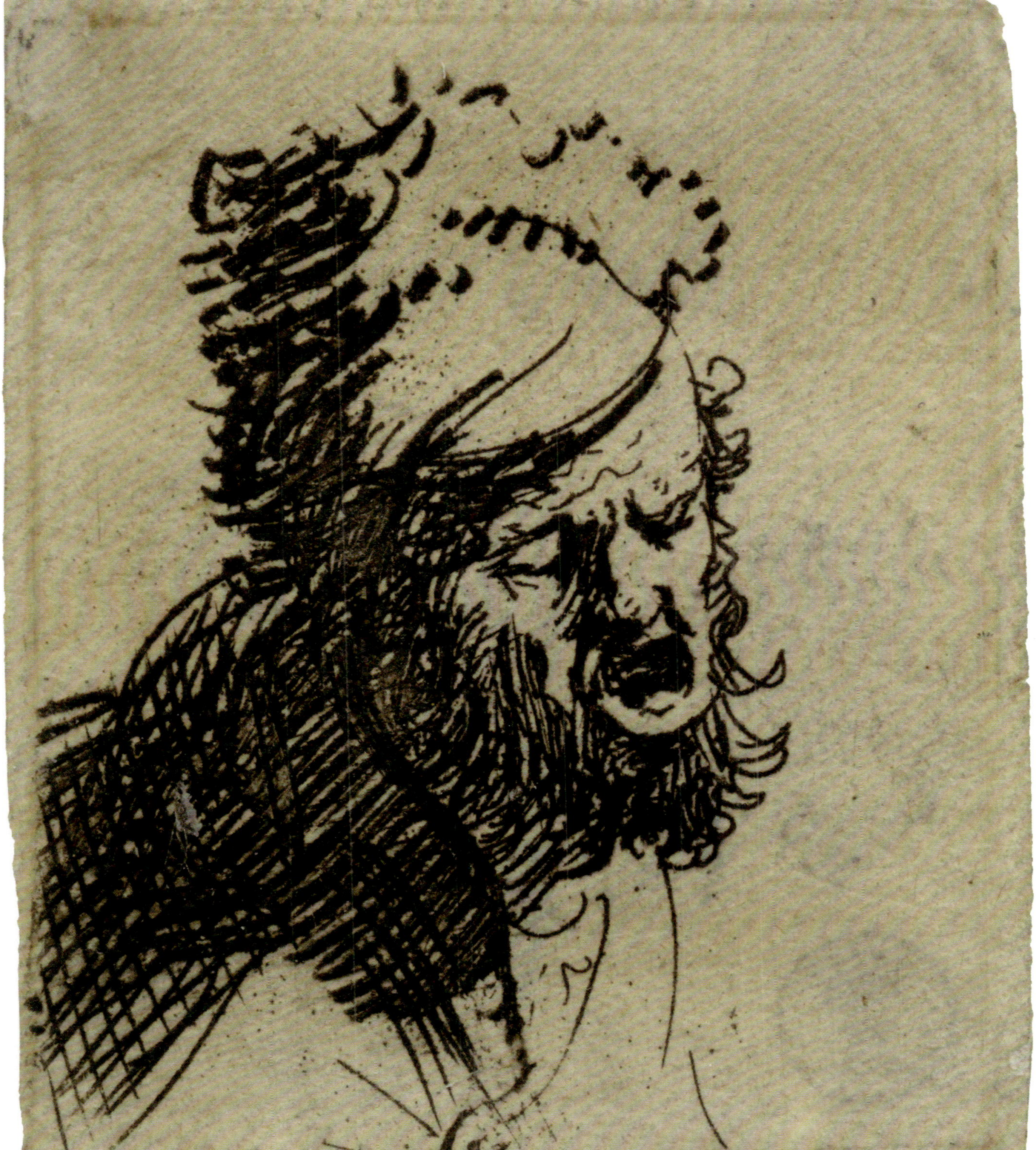

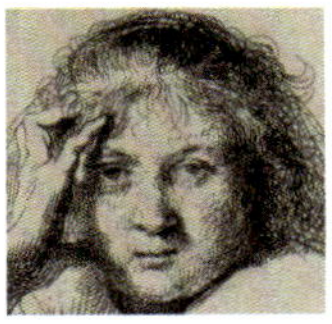

The White Negress (III/III), 1630
Etching on paper
9.8 x 7.8 cm
NWHCM : 1951.47.3

This bust-length portrait of an unknown, well-dressed young woman has had some doubts expressed by scholars in the past concerning its attribution. However, there are two impressions of this plate in the British Museum's collections which are printed on the verso of other etchings known to be by Rembrandt himself, so the attribution to him appears reliable.

The subject, who seems to be an albino woman of African heritage, would have been likely to be of interest to Rembrandt, offering the unusual artistic challenge of depicting in monochrome a subject who combined African features with pale skin. Rembrandt would have seen black people living in Amsterdam. Evidence exists of both free and enslaved people in this large and cosmopolitan city from the early seventeenth century (see Dienke Hondius, 'Blacks in Early Modern Europe', in Darlene Clark Hine, Trica Danielle Keaton and Stephen Small, eds., *Black Europe and the African Diaspora*, Urbana and Chicago, University of Illinois Press, 2009, p.42).

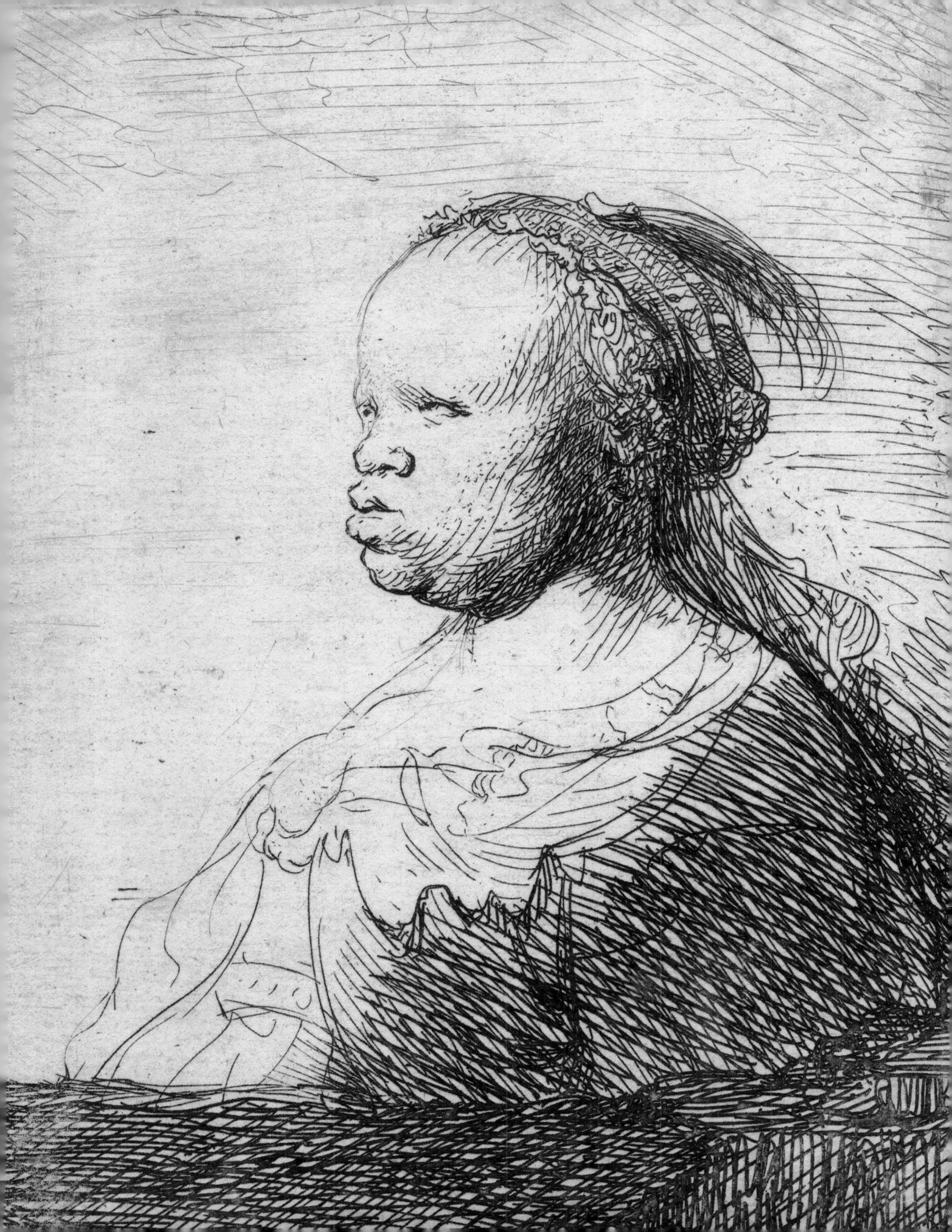

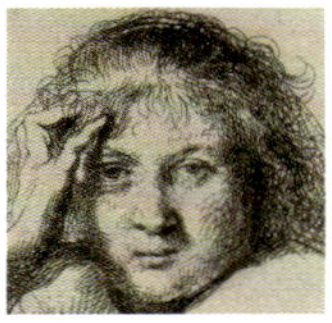

Three Heads of Women, one lightly Etched (III/III), 1637
Etching retouched with brush and grey ink on paper
12.7 x 10.2 cm
NWHCM : 1951.47.21

Saskia van Uylenburgh (1612-1642) married Rembrandt in 1634. She was from a wealthy family, the niece of Rembrandt's first employer, artist and dealer Hendrik Uylenburgh. During the eight years of their marriage, Rembrandt portrayed Saskia in paint, drawing and print, many times and in many poses from the formal to the homely and domestic. Other images of her may be seen on p.9 and p.25.

It was popular at the time for printmakers to publish studies of the heads of their models in different poses, often in a variety of headgear, as here. However, the first state of this print included only one view of Saskia. For the second state Rembrandt added both the view of her looking down, and the rudimentarily suggested third view, in which only her eyes are delineated in any detail. He was clearly aiming to capture the immediacy of a page of sketches, although as with all Rembrandt's printed 'sketches' his re-working of the plates shows that they were far more finished, even if the overall result was one of informality. In portraits like this one, the sketch-like format aids in creating the feeling of intimacy with the subject. Rembrandt captures the essence of his wife's plump, pretty face and pleasant expression, while the three views of her in close proximity add to the effect of three-dimensionality, as if he is exploring her face at all angles, moving her between one pose and another.

After the strong shading Rembrandt uses to define Saskia's face on the first two heads, the third view, so palely sketched as to be almost invisible, is a surprising contrast. Rembrandt seems to have been experimenting at just how minimal a face could be and still remain a recognisable portrait. Perhaps here he is telling us that the eyes, which express so much of a sitter's personality, must be the starting point and the bare minimum. Thus this portrait of Saskia's eyes is full of character: she stares directly out at the viewer, enigmatic and thoughtful. Even though they are her only clearly illustrated feature, her eyes ensure she is very much present in this portrait.

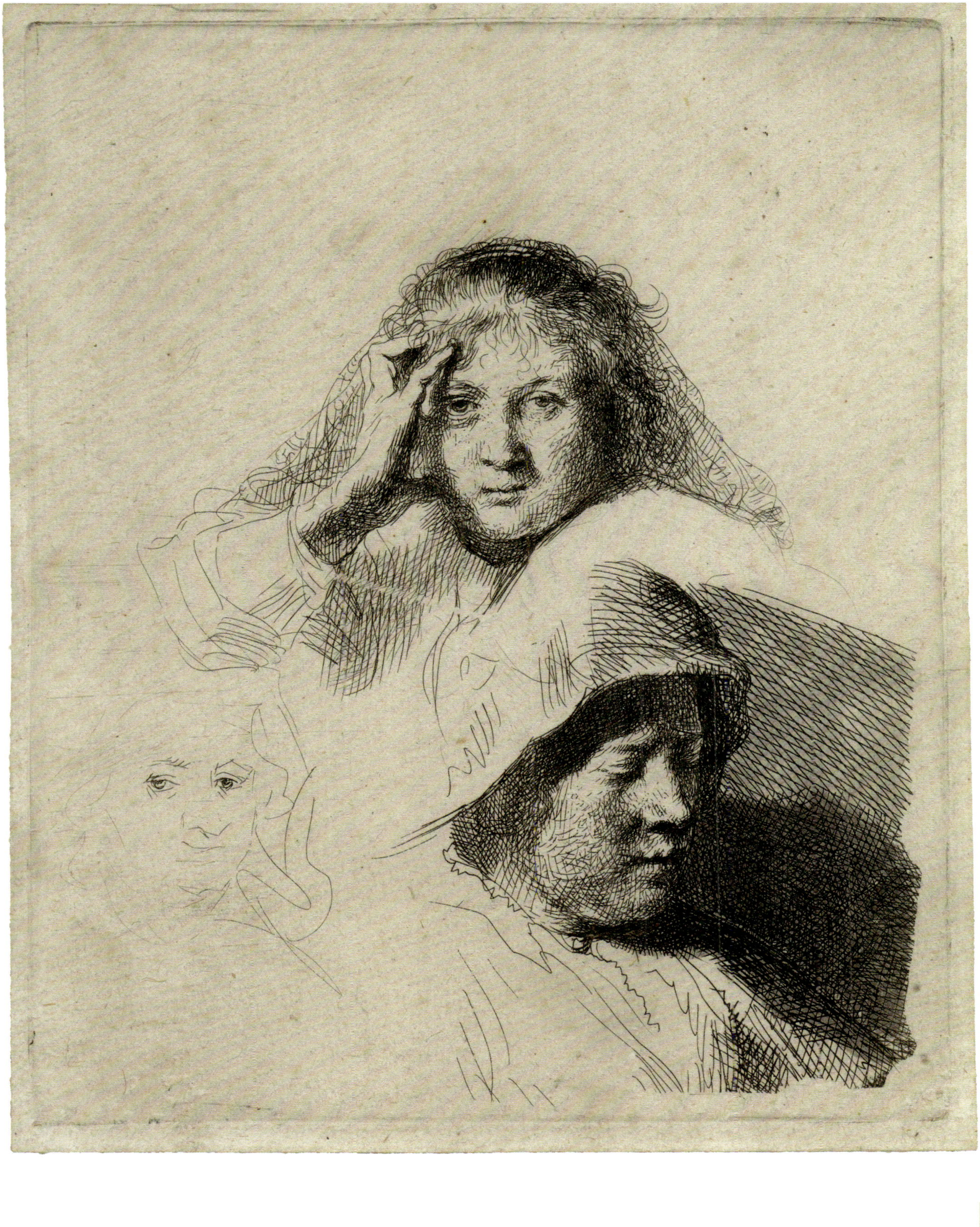

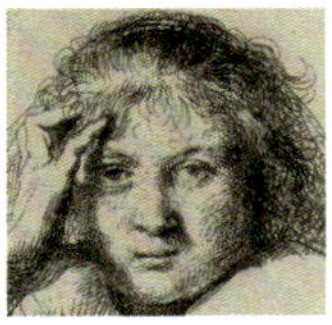

Old Man with a divided fur Cap (I/II), 1640
Etching and drypoint on paper
14.9 x 13.7 cm
Signed and dated in plate upper left of subject 'Rembrandt f / 1640'
NWHCM : 1951.47.28

Rembrandt's genius in depicting faces was never more notable than in his many portraits of older people. This unknown old man wears a large fur cap, of a Polish style known as a *kutschma*, headgear which appears elsewhere in Rembrandt's work, so may have belonged to the artist rather than the sitter. In this print, tilted at a rakish angle, it is the beautifully depicted hat that first draws the eye. The texture of the fur is communicated with fine, painterly shading, contrasting with the old man's equally finely drawn hair and bushy beard.

The hat, combined with the suggestion of a chain across his chest, imparts an air of status and weighty dignity to this sitter. However, as with all Rembrandt's portraits, the individual's personality is paramount, with all its positives and negatives, and glimpses of the possibilities of what may have happened in that person's life to give them their present identity.

In this print, lost in his own thoughts, the old man's gaze is directed away from the viewer, inviting questions as to what he is looking at and thinking about. The heavy eyebrows and keen, serious expression in the dark eyes contrast with the pouchiness of the deep bags under his eyes and the wrinkles in his forehead. All of these suggest age, tiredness and tension, the latter emphasised by the knotted hand clenched in front of him. His large bulbous nose shows clear signs of a past break. His beard, like that of many old men, grows half over his face and his visible ear seems to be sporting a wart. Rembrandt's faces are not beautiful. Above all, they are 'lived-in', and despite the gap of almost four hundred years, they are timeless. This old man could at any moment turn his head and speak to us.

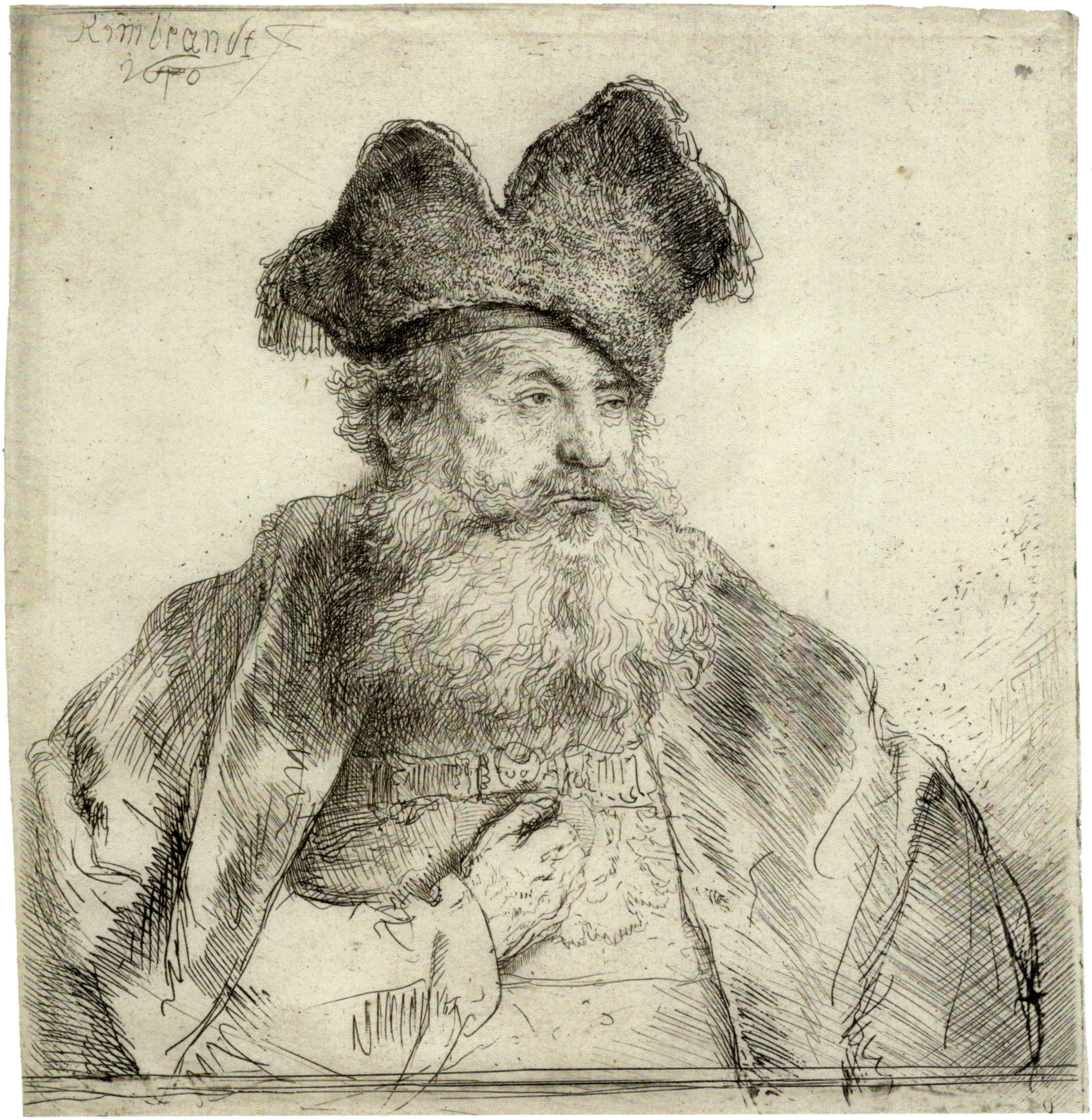
Rembrandt

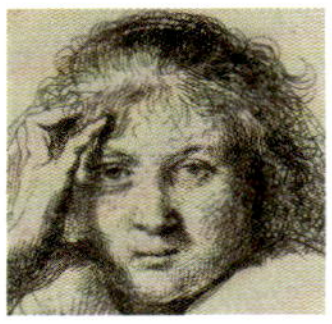

The Blindness of Tobit: The larger Plate (I/II), 1651
Etching and drypoint on paper
16.1 x 13 cm
Signed and dated twice in plate lower centre 'Rembrandt f. 1651' and lower right 'Rembrandt f 1651'
NWHCM : 1951.47.58

This print depicts a scene from the Book of Tobit. This book is part of the Apocrypha, historically not considered appropriate for inclusion in the mainstream Bible by all authorities, although Tobit did appear in the Dutch Protestant Bible Rembrandt would have known. The themes of this short book were depicted by Rembrandt more than any from other books of the Bible, so the story must have been particularly appealing to him. The story involves a righteous man, Tobit, struck blind. His son Tobias, away in a foreign land, is guided by the angel Raphael to destroy a demon who has cursed his new wife, Sarah, by murdering all her seven previous husbands. Tobias drives out the demon and returns home, where, again on the advice of the angel, he restores his father's sight.

Rembrandt had a particular interest in portraying the condition of blindness. There is a possibility that his own father may have been blind: a drawing from the Ashmolean Museum labelled with Rembrandt's father's name (*Portrait of the Artist's Father, Harmen Gerritsz. van Rijn*) appears to portray a blind man. This personal connection may have given Rembrandt a sympathy with the blind, or at least an artistic curiosity in portraying the condition. Blind people appear many times over throughout Rembrandt's work. Apart from Tobit he portrayed biblical characters Samson, Simeon and Jacob, classical figures Homer (*Homer*, 1663, Mauritshuis, The Hague) and Claudius Civilis (*The Conspiracy of the Batavians under Claudius Civilis*, c.1661, Royal Academy of Fine Arts, Sweden), and others.

In this print Tobit has been waiting for his son, who has been away so long he is feared dead. Tobit has just heard someone at the door and blunders towards the sound. In his haste, although his dog tries to guide him, he has knocked over a spinning wheel and missed the door. Rembrandt's interpretation follows a passage in the Dutch Bible of his time, which includes a poignant detail of Tobit hitting himself against the door as he tries to find it.

As well as a biblical subject, this etching is a realistic and moving portrait. The old man's face, at the centre of the composition, draws the eye compellingly. The deeply shadowed hollows of his eyes and his sunken cheeks, combined with the outstretched hand, convey eloquently the darkness in which he is trapped: both the physical darkness of his world and the spiritual darkness of his grief at, so he believes, the loss of Tobias.

Rembrandt excelled at portraying the precise moment of a character's enlightenment – in all senses of the word. The viewer knows that Tobit's misfortunes are a split second away from miraculous reversal through divine intervention. But Tobit himself is an entirely human portrait of vulnerability, and of despair at the turning point of transformation into hope.

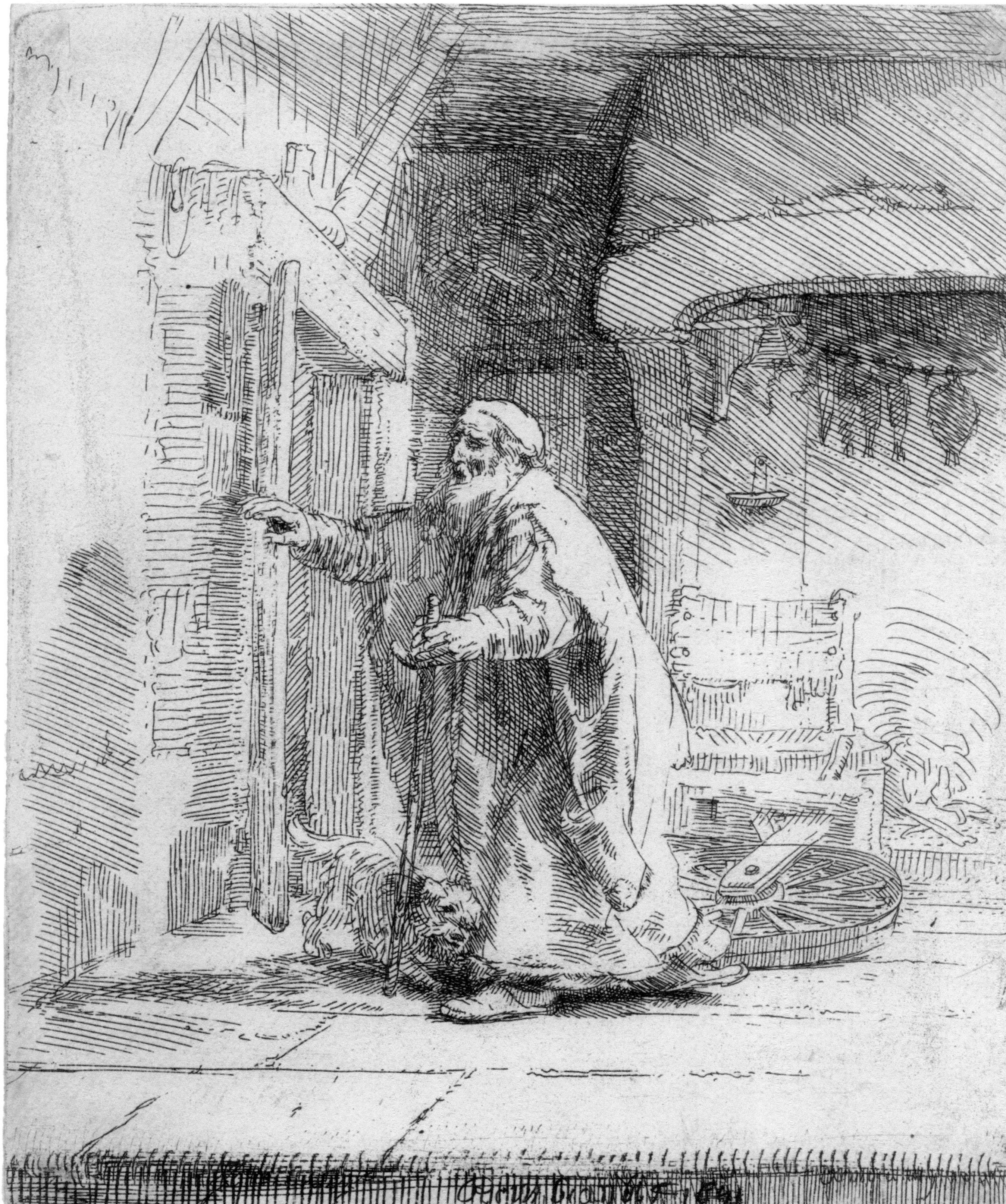

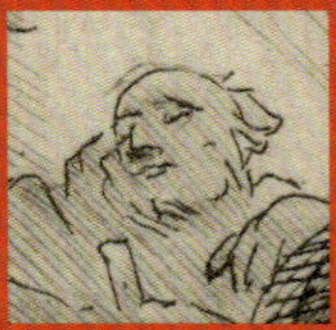

Behold the Man

In seventeenth-century Dutch art, religious subjects were less fashionable than still lifes, landscapes and genre scenes. However, a large proportion of Rembrandt's print output consisted of religious works: over eighty in total. Holland was Protestant, rather than Catholic like much of the rest of Europe at that time, which allowed the artist a different approach. Rather than a Catholic emphasis on depictions of saints and miracles, Rembrandt's religious subjects are taken from the Bible, many from the Old Testament, some from the Apocrypha.

True to his love of realism, Rembrandt portrayed his religious figures in contemporary dress and surroundings. Certain themes he interpreted many times over in different ways: the stories of Tobit, Tobias and Sarah, Abraham and Isaac. He was particularly drawn to exploring situations in which ordinary people are transformed through contact with the divine. Even for a viewer today, with a far more secular outlook than Rembrandt's contemporaries would have had, these scenes have the power to move. His best-known prints include scenes from the life and death of Jesus. The theme of Christ's Passion had been treated frequently in Northern European art by Rembrandt's time. Among other artists Albrecht Dürer (1471-1528) and Lucas van Leyden (1494-1533), whose works Rembrandt admired and collected, had both produced celebrated sets of engravings on this subject, which influenced Rembrandt.

However, Rembrandt's approach differed to that of earlier masters. He clearly saw biblical subjects as a rich opportunity to explore human intimacy alongside religious devotion. He used light and darkness in these works with a particular purpose to combine the human with the divine, drawing the viewer in to participate in the emotions experienced by the characters within the narrative.

Interpreting Jesus' death and burial as a 'dark night of the soul' for humanity led Rembrandt to depict this subject in some of the darkest prints he ever made. This technically daring, artistically stunning blackness emphasises tragedy and despair, but a source of light is always visible somewhere in the composition, however small, as a reminder of the ever-present possibility of divine grace and the human capacity for redemption.

The Angel Appearing to the Shepherds (III/IV), 1634
Etching, engraving and drypoint on paper
25.9 x 22 cm
Signed and dated in plate lower right of subject 'Rembrandt f. 1634'
NWHCM : 1951.47.9

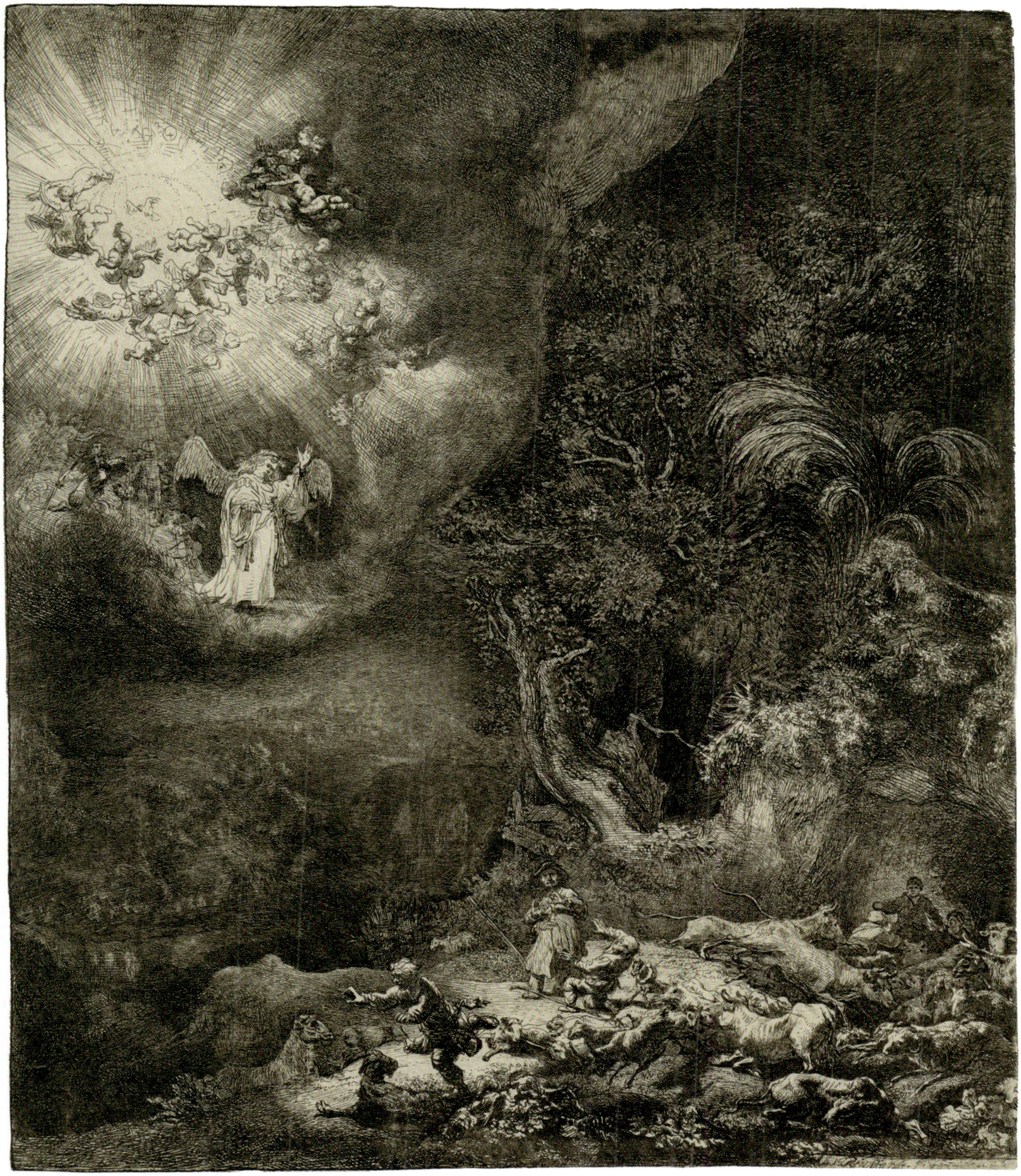

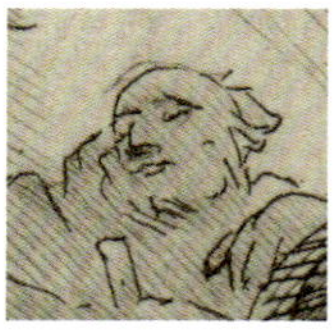

The Flight into Egypt: Crossing a Brook (only state), 1654
Etching, engraving and drypoint on paper
9.4 x 14.4 cm
Signed and dated in plate lower left of subject 'Rembrandt f. 1654'
NWHCM : 1951.47.76

Here Mary and Joseph are depicted leaving for Egypt just after Jesus' birth, to avoid King Herod's orders to kill all first-born boys, the 'Massacre of the Innocents' recounted in the Gospel of Matthew. The Bible account is brief, saying nothing of the details of the Holy Family's journey. However, the subject is perennially popular in art: before Rembrandt numerous great artists, including Michelangelo da Caravaggio (1571-1610), Annibale Carracci (1560-1609), Albrecht Dürer (1471-1533) and Peter Paul Rubens (1577-1640) had portrayed aspects of this story, many of which Rembrandt would have known through prints. The closest in spirit to Rembrandt's interpretation is probably that of Dürer, whose woodcut *The Flight into Egypt* (1511) shows the Holy Family, Joseph carrying their possessions, Mary and Jesus on the donkey, in a woodland setting. Nonetheless, Rembrandt studies the human dimension far more deeply than any of his predecessors.

This print is Rembrandt's second treatment of the subject. In the first version, *The Flight into Egypt: a Night Piece* (1651) (see p.7), Rembrandt portrayed the Holy Family at night, re-working the plate several times to decrease the light, creating a darker background with each re-working until only the barest outlines of the figures remain visible by a tiny point of light from Joseph's lamp.

In this second interpretation, Rembrandt was aiming at a different effect. He still shows the scene in relative darkness, enough to emphasise the secrecy of their escape, but with sufficient light remaining to allow a close-up focus on the characters and their situation. The faces, the donkey's fur, the clothing, the trees and the brook are all rendered with perfect clarity, right down to Joseph's battered, lopsided hat. All this contributes to the realism of the scene.

Many of the interpretations by other artists include angels within the composition, coming down from heaven to guide the family onwards. In this print there is no such obvious divine aid close at hand. We are just shown a vivid snapshot of an ordinary family: tired, dispirited and vulnerably alone. The word 'flight' gives the impression of swift escape, but Rembrandt reminds us that the Holy Family's journey, plodding along with their donkey, would in reality have been anything but.

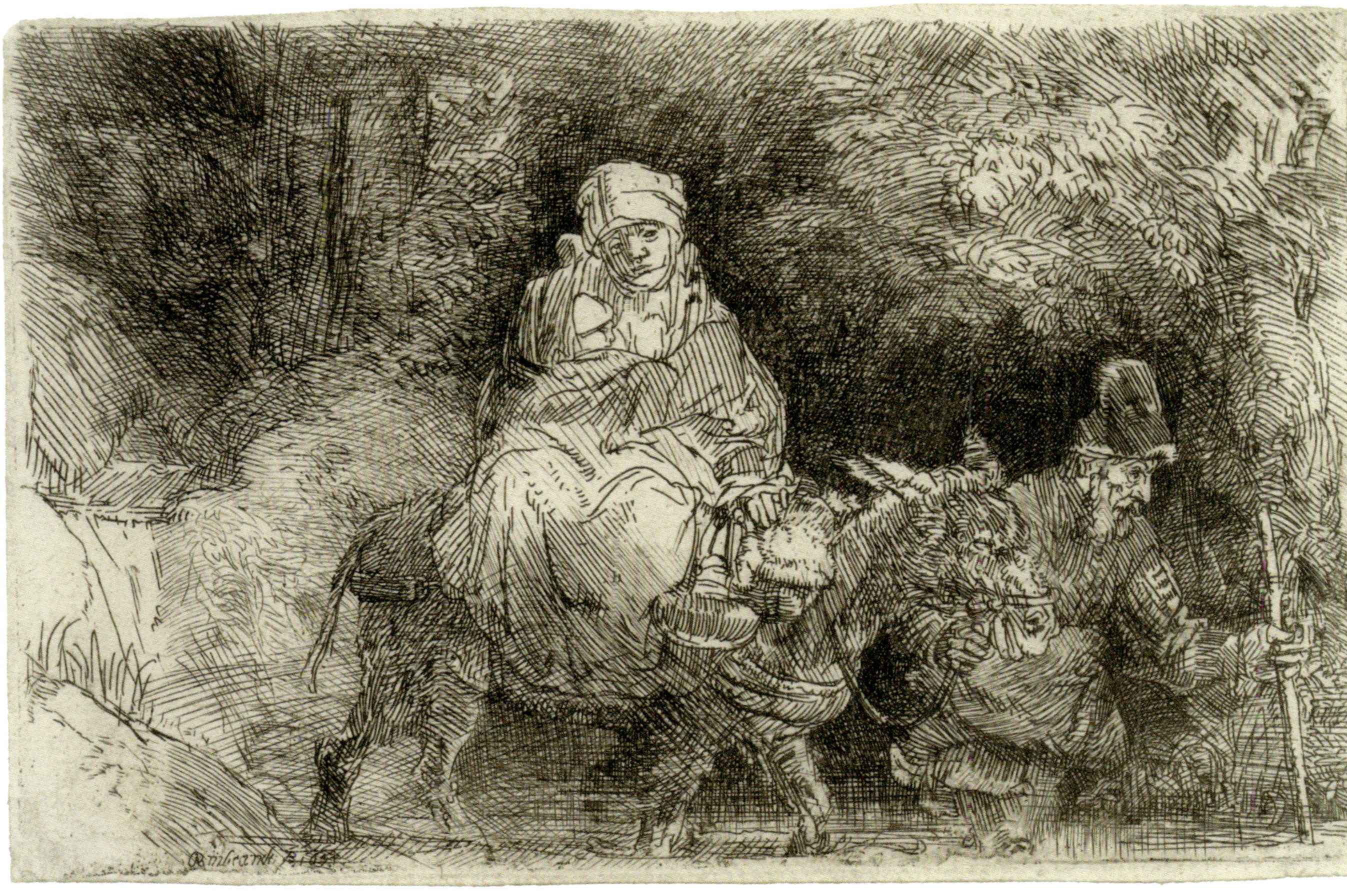

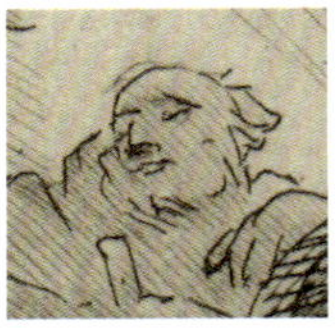

Christ, with the Sick around Him, Receiving little Children. 'The Hundred Guilder Print' (II/IV), 1648
Etching, engraving and drypoint on paper
27.8 x 38.9 cm
NWHCM : 1951.47.51

This was and remains one of Rembrandt's best-known prints. The name 'One Hundred Guilder Print' was a contemporary one, referring to its expense. One hundred guilders would have been the average equivalent of a month's salary for a middle class Dutchman at the time. This high price indicates how sought-after Rembrandt's prints were during his lifetime.

Artistically and technically the work is strikingly original. Rembrandt used drypoint to achieve what was then a very new artistic effect, creating a far wider range of tints and shades of blacks and subtle greys than was possible through either engraving or etching alone. Scratching directly with the burin onto the copper plate rather than through an etching ground produced more burr, in which the ink would catch, therefore making the edges of the lines softer, creating a more painterly look.

The subject matter is a series of events from the life of Jesus from chapter 19 of St Matthew's Gospel, interwoven into one composition. Rembrandt used a much wider plate than his usual ones to bring all the elements of the narrative together. Although not placed at the centre of the print Jesus commands attention through his upright posture surrounded by a dark background, combined with his very finely drawn and shaded halo, which lights up the area immediately behind his head and illuminates his face and outstretched hands. As if he is radiating light, the shadow of the uplifted hands of the kneeling man begging for his help is reflected on his robe. With his left hand Jesus is about to bless the sick who are placed in attitudes of supplication before him, their long line stretching through and beyond the dimly-lit doorway to the right. The queue of people waiting seems endless, perhaps signalling to a Christian viewer that humanity's need for God is also endless.

With his right hand, Jesus encourages a mother to bring her child to him for blessing while, behind them, another child gestures towards Jesus, pulling his mother forward. To the far left a group of Pharisees sit at a table, their back to Jesus, debating how best to catch him out with questions. Between the Pharisees and the women sits a dejected-looking young man with long hair and fine clothes, his hand to his forehead. He may be the rich man whom Jesus has told that the best way to salvation is to give away all his wealth. The camel's head just visible in semi-darkness, peering round the door to the right, may also refer to this story: it being easier for a camel to pass through the eye of a needle than for a rich man to enter the kingdom of heaven.

Rembrandt's audience would have been familiar with all these stories. The superb interweaving of narratives, and the beautifully-portrayed individual details for each of the many people in this print explain its enduring popularity, as Rembrandt brought his combination of sharply-observed realism and empathetic humanity to the scene, giving it universal appeal.

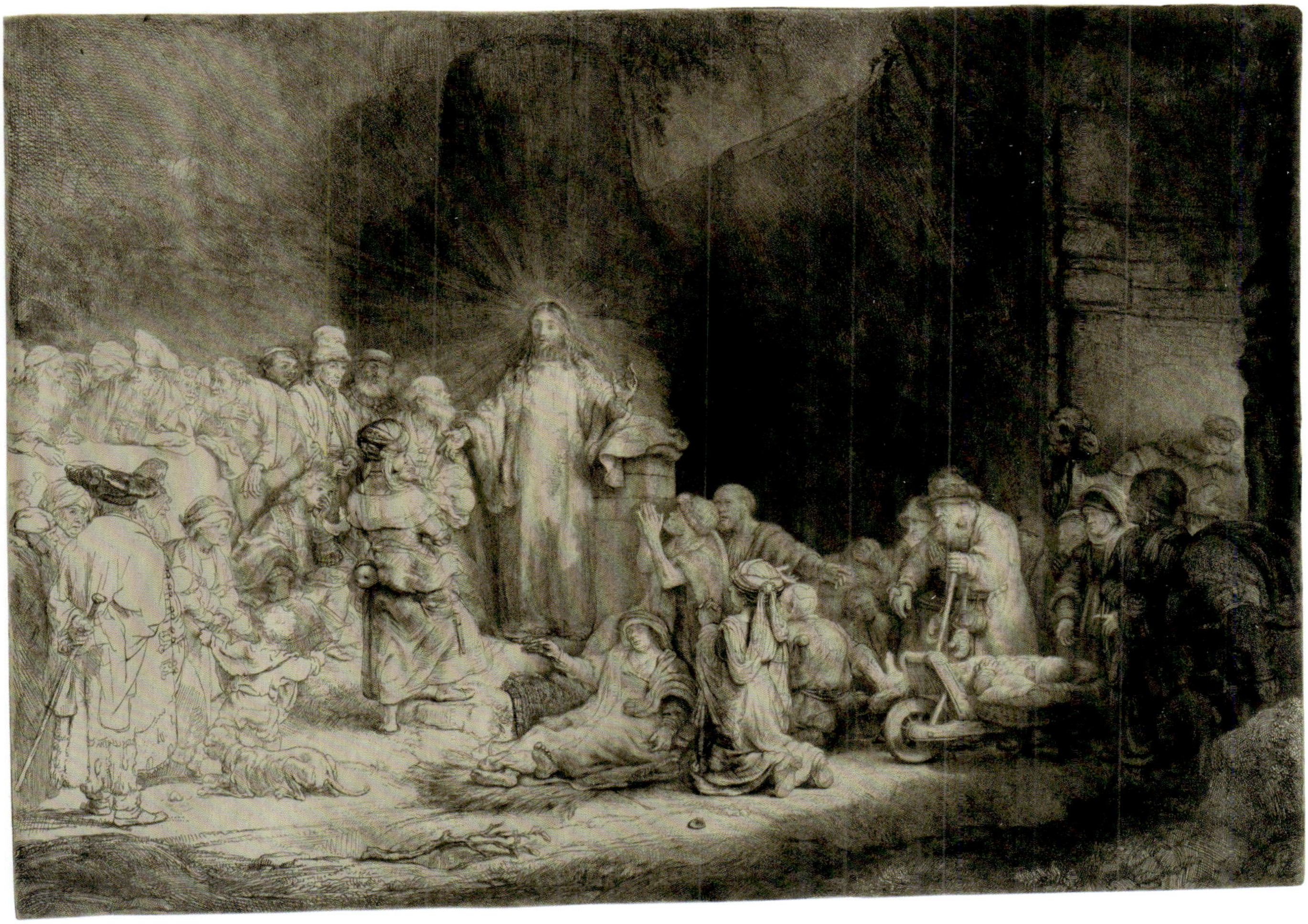

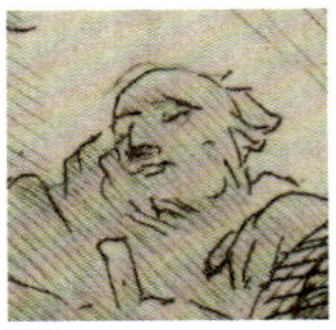

The Agony in the Garden (I/III), c.1654-57
Etching and drypoint on paper
11.1 x 8.4 cm
Signed and dated in plate lower right of subject 'Rembrandt f. 165...'
NWHCM : 1951.47.90

Like many of his scenes from the Passion, Rembrandt has chosen to portray this interpretation of the Agony in the Garden of Gethsemane in dramatically dark tones. This scene represents the 'dark night of the soul' for Jesus himself. He prays in anguish, with three of his disciples, Peter, James and John, sketched to the left in just enough detail to show that they are fast asleep, oblivious to the situation. Further in the background, a crowd of people is ominously visible: we are aware that Jesus' arrest and condemnation are not far away. The black shadowed shapes representing Jerusalem and the night sky loom oppressively above, a portent of the coming storm. The bold diagonal lines scored across the print might also suggest sheeting rain, light from heaven heralding the arrival of the angel, or simply be intended to add to the atmosphere of urgency and the sense of impending crisis.

As well as this print (this first state the only one entirely in the artist's hand without posthumous alterations), Rembrandt made several drawings of the subject, experimenting with the positioning of the figures of Jesus and the angel within the composition. Here he has chosen to portray the kneeling angel in profile, and position Jesus facing the viewer. This places greater emphasis on Jesus although, like the faces of the sleeping disciples his face is not portrayed in any detail. Despite his extraordinary abilities at depicting faces, Rembrandt here chooses to convey the sense of Jesus' profound sadness more through the angle of his head and the placing of the shadows than focusing closely on his facial features. Jesus' eyes are closed and in this way Rembrandt suggests that he has not yet seen or felt the angel's arrival. He is still locked in despairing loneliness: his fear that he has been forsaken by God. We as viewers know that this darkness of suffering will only be temporary, that God has come to his aid, but at this precise moment Jesus himself is still, literally and metaphorically, in the dark. As ever, Rembrandt has found the human angle to balance with the portrayal of divine intervention, showing Jesus at his lowest ebb.

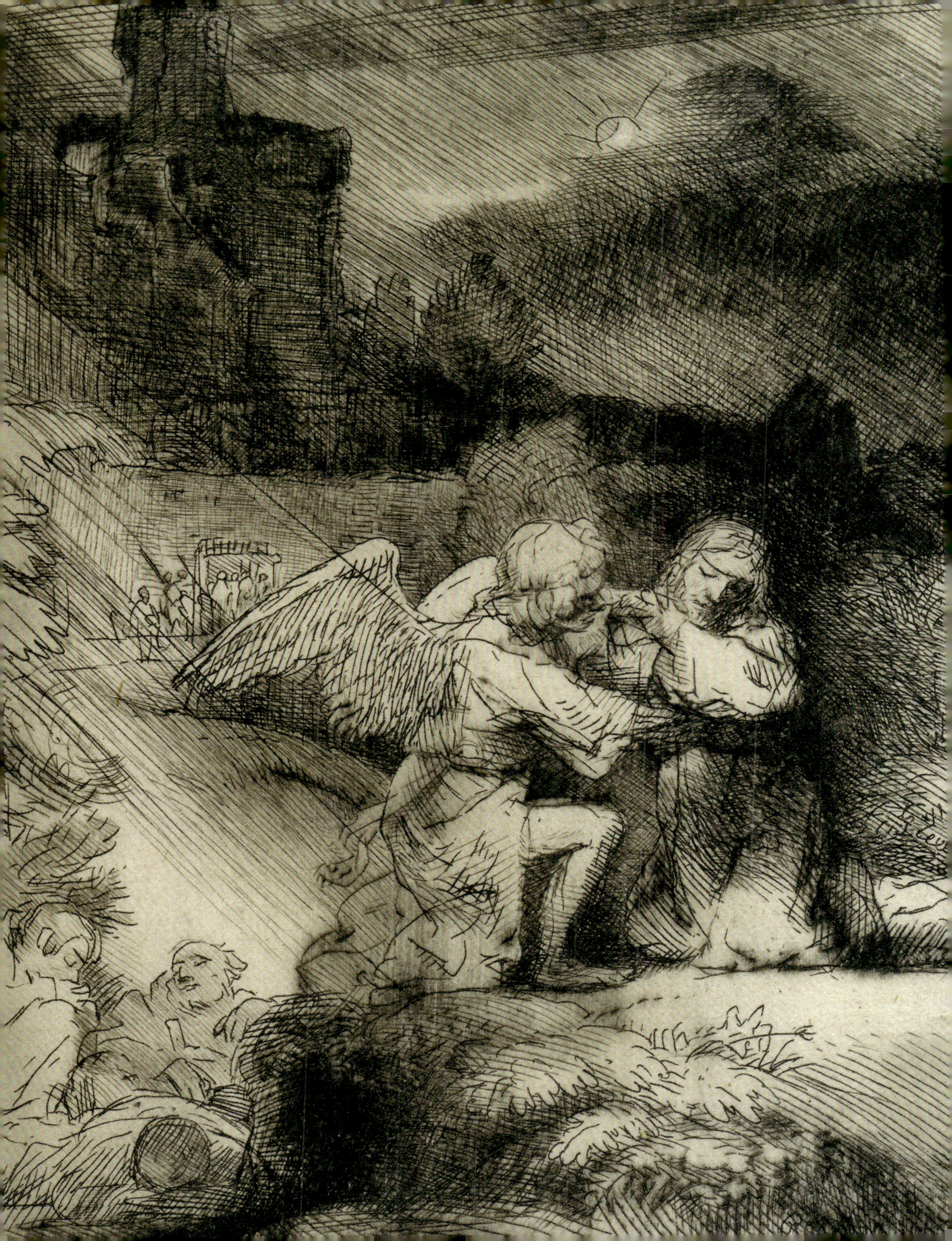

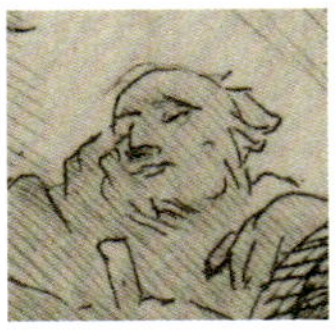

Christ Presented to the People: Oblong Plate (V/VIII), 1655
Drypoint on vellum
34.8 x 43.6 cm
NWHCM : 1951.47.84

The initial inspiration for one of Rembrandt's best and most famous prints was a version of the subject by Lucas van Leyden (1494-1533). Rembrandt greatly admired the work of this masterly printmaker from his own home town of Leiden, and reportedly paid the vast sum of 1,400 guilders for an album of van Leyden's prints, which included his version of *Christ Presented to the People*, made in 1510. It was also known as *Ecce Homo*, 'Behold the Man', traditionally what Pontius Pilate said when he displayed Jesus to the crowd.

The basic elements of Rembrandt's print closely resemble those of van Leyden. Pilate is presenting the captive Jesus to a motley crowd, on a raised dais within a city landscape, flanked by soldiers and surrounded by people looking on from their windows. However, in van Leyden's interpretation the superbly rendered architecture takes up at least half the picture plane, showing Jesus at a distance and making him a relatively small part of the composition. Rembrandt, on the other hand, crops out most of the cityscape, focusing, like a photographer with a zoom lens, much more closely on Jesus and the people around him.

Rembrandt made eight states of this print, and it is one in which his experimental approach is at its clearest and most interesting. As numerous other prints demonstrate, Rembrandt produced spectacular crowd scenes. Every individual, even if no larger than a few millimetres, is rendered with character and purpose, contributing to the meaning of the work. In this print however, for the sixth state he erased the people in front of the dais completely from the plate, leaving only those at either side. The foreground became first an empty space and, by the seventh state, had become two brick arches leading to tunnels of blackness. He also changed the structure of the architecture several times, bringing the focus in ever more tightly and dramatically on Jesus.

The print seen here is the fifth state, the last before the crowd was erased, although the plate had already changed in several ways since the first version. Rembrandt had begun to alter the architectural features, creating a more enclosed atmosphere and bringing the viewer's gaze nearer to Jesus on the dais.

Part of the reason for reworking the front of the plate after this version was purely technical: the burr of metal created by the drypoint needle, which produces velvety-edged lines where the ink catches, had begun to wear so that the effect was not as striking as on earlier states. Some re-working was necessary to retain the print's quality. Nonetheless, Rembrandt turned this to artistic advantage and used it as an experimental opportunity.

This print is the only one in Norwich Castle's collection to be printed on vellum. This support is much less absorbent than paper, which results in more ink remaining on the surface. This effect, combined with the burr of the drypoint needle and the golden colour of the vellum creates a rich, painterly look of depth and character.

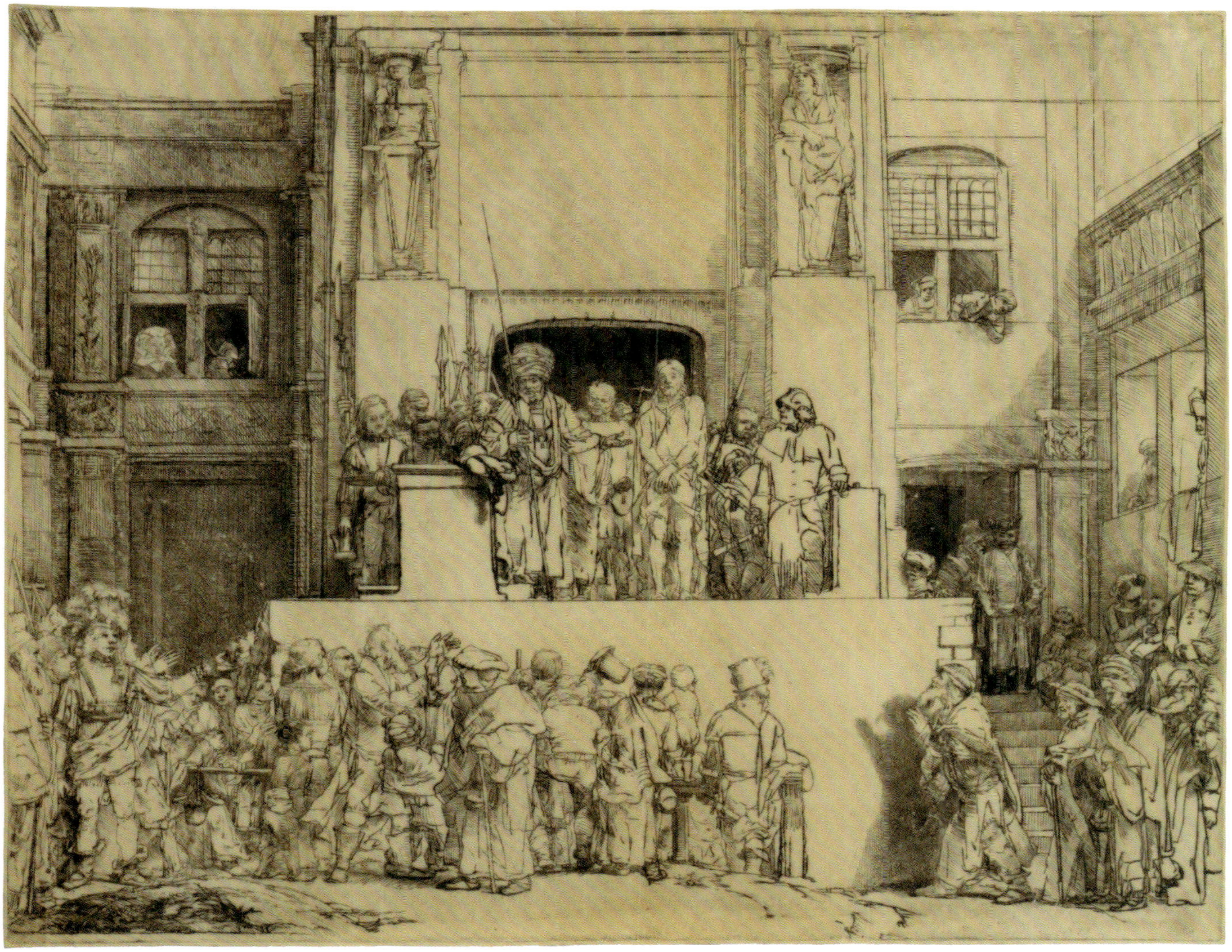

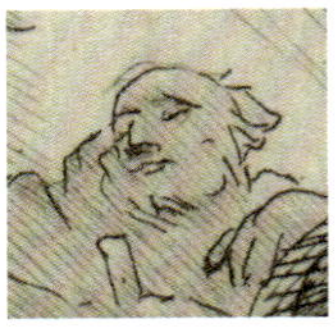

The Descent from the Cross, a Sketch (only state), 1642
Etching and drypoint on paper
14.9 x 11.6 cm
Signed and dated in plate lower right of subject 'Rembrandt f. 1642'
NWHCM : 1951.47.39

In Rembrandt's lifetime, the most famous image of Jesus' body being taken down from the Cross (this stage of the Passion also known as the Deposition) would have been the monumental altarpiece produced by Peter Paul Rubens (1577-1640) for Antwerp cathedral in 1612. This was a stunningly dramatic Baroque work which would have been familiar to Rembrandt in print form. Rembrandt himself tackled this subject several times during his career, and was clearly influenced by Rubens. The first of his portrayals of the Deposition formed part of a commission around 1632, which comprised a series of five paintings on the theme of Christ's Passion, for one of his most important early patrons, Prince Frederick Hendrick of Orange.

However, in this interpretation Rembrandt seems to be intent less on the religious nature or the drama of the story and more on exploring the mechanics of just how a dead body would be removed after crucifixion. The traditional elements of the scene are incorporated, including the swooning Virgin Mary, the discarded crown of thorns, and the skull and bones beneath the Cross, a reference to the place name Golgotha, the 'place of a skull', but the main emphasis is on the mundane details. In Rubens' Deposition the dead Christ is held and lowered in a white shroud which forms a drapery to frame the tortuous pose of the body. Rembrandt's version also features a shroud, although here it is less picturesquely but more practically looped under Jesus' arms to support the dead weight of the corpse and stop it from falling forwards once the nails in the hands are removed. To the left, a lightly etched workman at the top of a ladder works with his pincers to pull the nail out from Jesus' right hand. A man on the ground behind the Cross on the other side, his arms taut with effort, holds both ends of the shroud to take the strain.

The pincers and ladder both feature in traditional Christian iconography among the instruments of Jesus' Passion, which include the crown of thorns, the scourge, the robe, the hammer and the lance among others. In Rembrandt's print they become everyday tools, no less grisly for being shown in use by the workman, as he matter-of-factly goes about the task of taking out the nails. If the tool sketched at his belt is a hammer, this workman may be the same man who originally drove them in.

The collector's mark to the left of Rembrandt's signature belongs to Martin Folkes (1690-1754), the earliest known collector of this print. A member and then President of the Royal Society and the Society of Antiquaries, Folkes collected books, paintings, coins, prints and drawings. The print was then in Vienna with the artist Joseph Daniel Böhm (1794-1865) and in the late nineteenth century belonged to the State Hermitage Museum in St Petersburg.

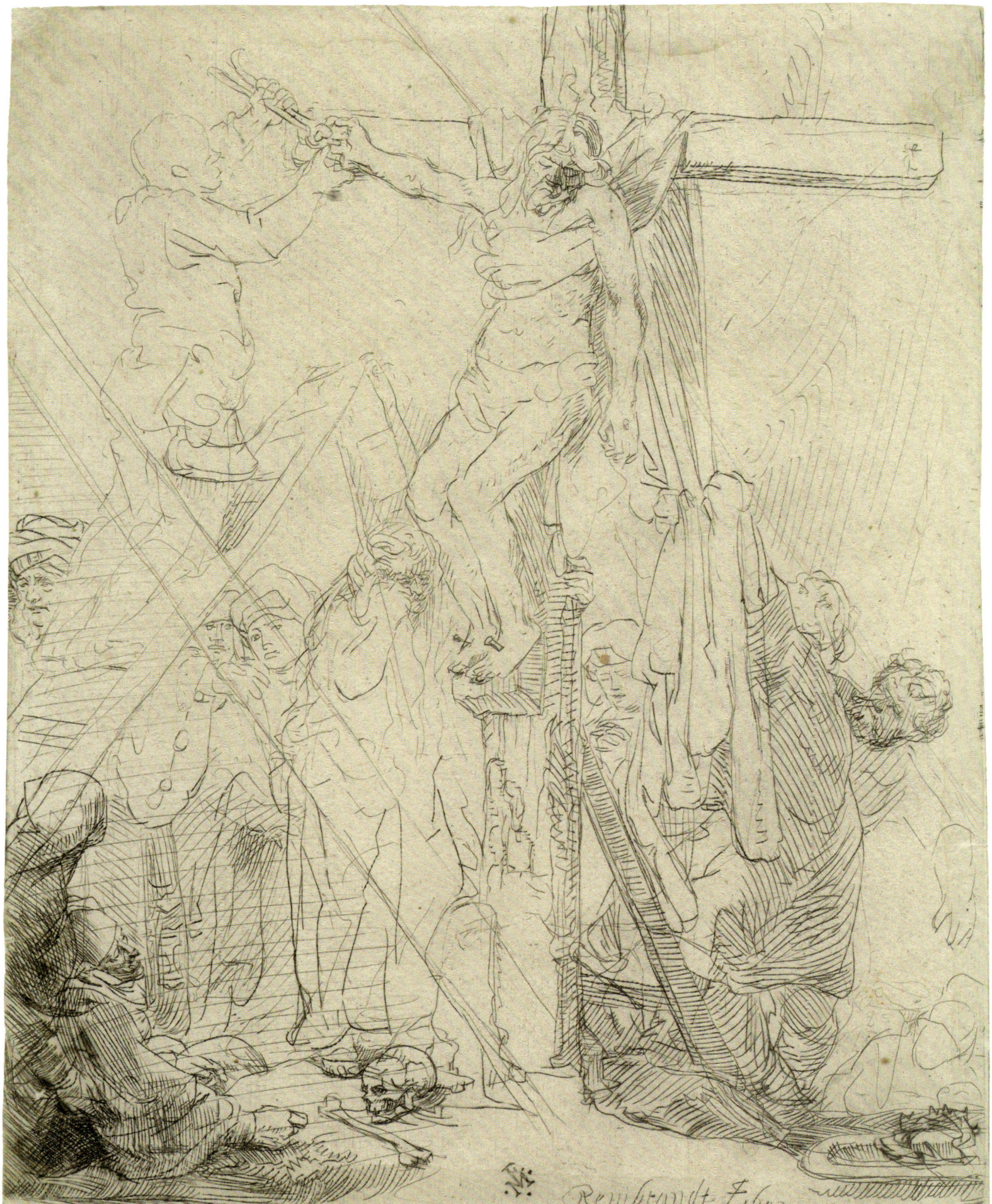
Rembrandt f. 1642

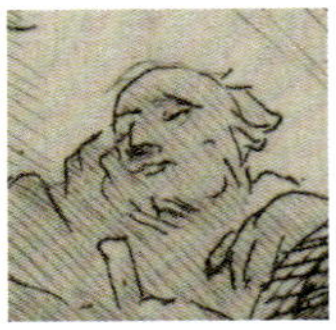

The Descent from the Cross by Torchlight (I/IV), 1654
Etching and drypoint on paper
21.1 x 16.1 cm
Signed and dated in plate lower centre left of subject
'Rembrandt. f 1654'
NWHCM : 1951.47.78

This is Rembrandt's second interpretation in print of the Deposition. Different details are highlighted, and different effects explored, compared with the version from 1642 on the previous page. The action takes place only a short time after the earlier print, but it is now night, with only the flickering light of a torch illuminating the scene. Jesus' hands and one of his feet have now been unfastened and his body has been lowered sideways, pivoting around the large nail which still pinions his right foot. This has presumably been left deliberately until the body has been taken down and is being supported at ground level. It would be easier to remove this final nail once there is no longer any weight pressing onto it.

The Cross itself is now scarcely visible, the focus of the action is shifting. The long line of the hanging shroud used to lower Jesus' body points diagonally downwards, leading the eye across the picture towards the bier upon which Joseph of Arimathea is laying another cloth, ready to receive the corpse. These two shrouds palely highlighted amid the gloom, vertical and horizontal, make a powerful visual pairing, connecting one part of the story to the next: from Crucifixion to Entombment.

The activity in this print is mostly happening in the upper left quarter of the composition. Jesus' body with its dangling legs and lolling head and arm provides the pivotal point around which the action moves. Just as in the earlier work, *Descent from the Cross: a Sketch,* Rembrandt shows us that getting a corpse down from a cross is no easy task. The man with his back to us stands braced, his bent knees and clenched calf muscles clearly demonstrating that he is taking most of the weight of the body, although there are several others helping, and the torchlight glints eerily on the outline of an outstretched hand, reaching up out of the darkness to catch the body should it slip.

The *chiaroscuro* of this night scene enhances these details visually by throwing them into sharp relief against the darkness, but it also increases the emotion and tragedy. The care all the men are taking to show reverence to the body reveals to the viewer that this is Jesus, no ordinary victim of this brutal but common Roman method of execution, but the very starkness of the portrayal has a timeless quality, revealing Rembrandt's sense of empathy with human suffering.

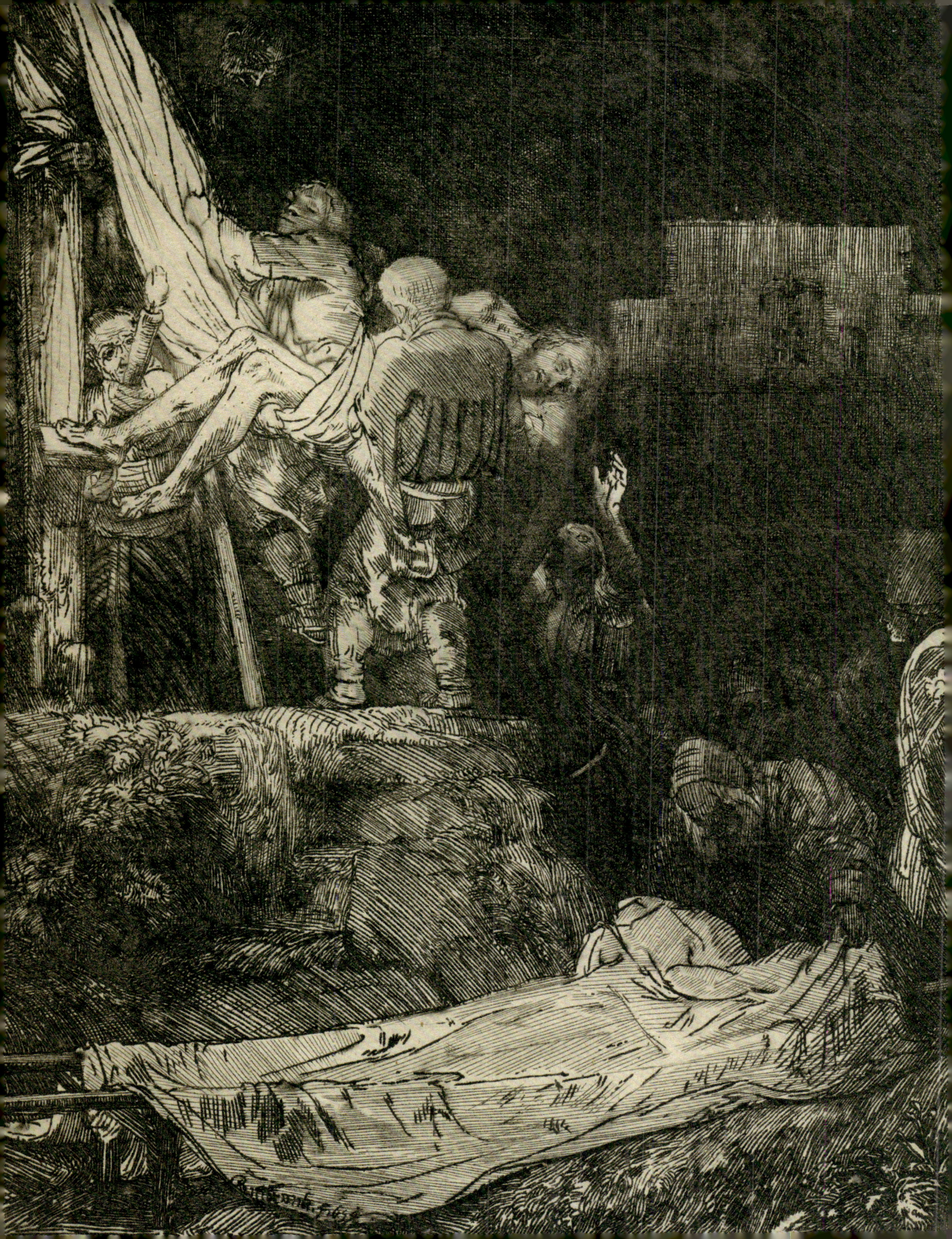

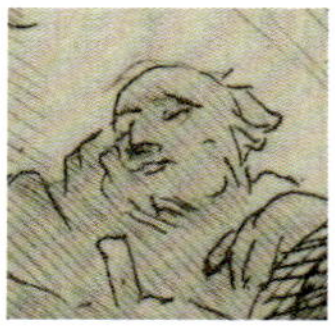

The Entombment (Night effect) (IV/IV), 1654
Etching and drypoint on paper
21.1 x 16.1 cm
NWHCM : 1951.47.83

Rembrandt portrayed this scene several times during the 1630s and 40s, in paintings, drawings and also in this later print, which has four states. For each state he dramatically darkened the plate. The first state uses only etching, but in subsequent states Rembrandt added extra shading in drypoint, to darken and blur all the details until, in the fourth state seen here, the figures are scarcely visible. It is clear that a candle is burning in the cavernous underground tomb, but the blackness is overwhelming, heavy and impenetrable. Even the two skulls, glimpsed on a ledge above the figures in the earlier states of the work, can no longer be seen.

Rembrandt makes it clear in this print that, for Mary and the other mourners, this is the end, the ultimate death. The almost complete darkness focuses our attention on the tomb and reflects the enormity of the events. Unlike the participants, the viewer knows that the Resurrection will follow in three days' time, but Rembrandt seems to be aiming for the viewer to feel that, at this moment, we are in the tomb with Christ, sharing in the weight of the despair shown on the faces of the Virgin and that of the deeply-lined man who may be Nicodemus, who brought spices to embalm the body and who sits at Christ's head, the faint light illuminating his white beard.

Rembrandt's renowned painting and his related oil sketch *The Entombment*, (c.1635-9, Alte Pinakothek, Munich, and c.1639, The Hunterian, University of Glasgow) use light and darkness with equally stunning drama. In both these works Rembrandt explores the effects of candlelight flickering within the dim interior of the tomb, achieving magnificently atmospheric results, but even the most restricted palette of colours gives a warmer appearance than this utterly uncompromising monochrome. In this work every extraneous detail has been erased: Rembrandt has literally sucked all the colour out of the mourners' world. They are left only with the cold, still blackness of grief.

At the turn of the nineteenth century this etching was in Vienna, in the collection of the great print connoisseur and curator of the Albertina Franz Rechberger (1771-1841). It was then in Dresden with Friedrich August II, King of Saxony, part of his collection of 110,000 prints.

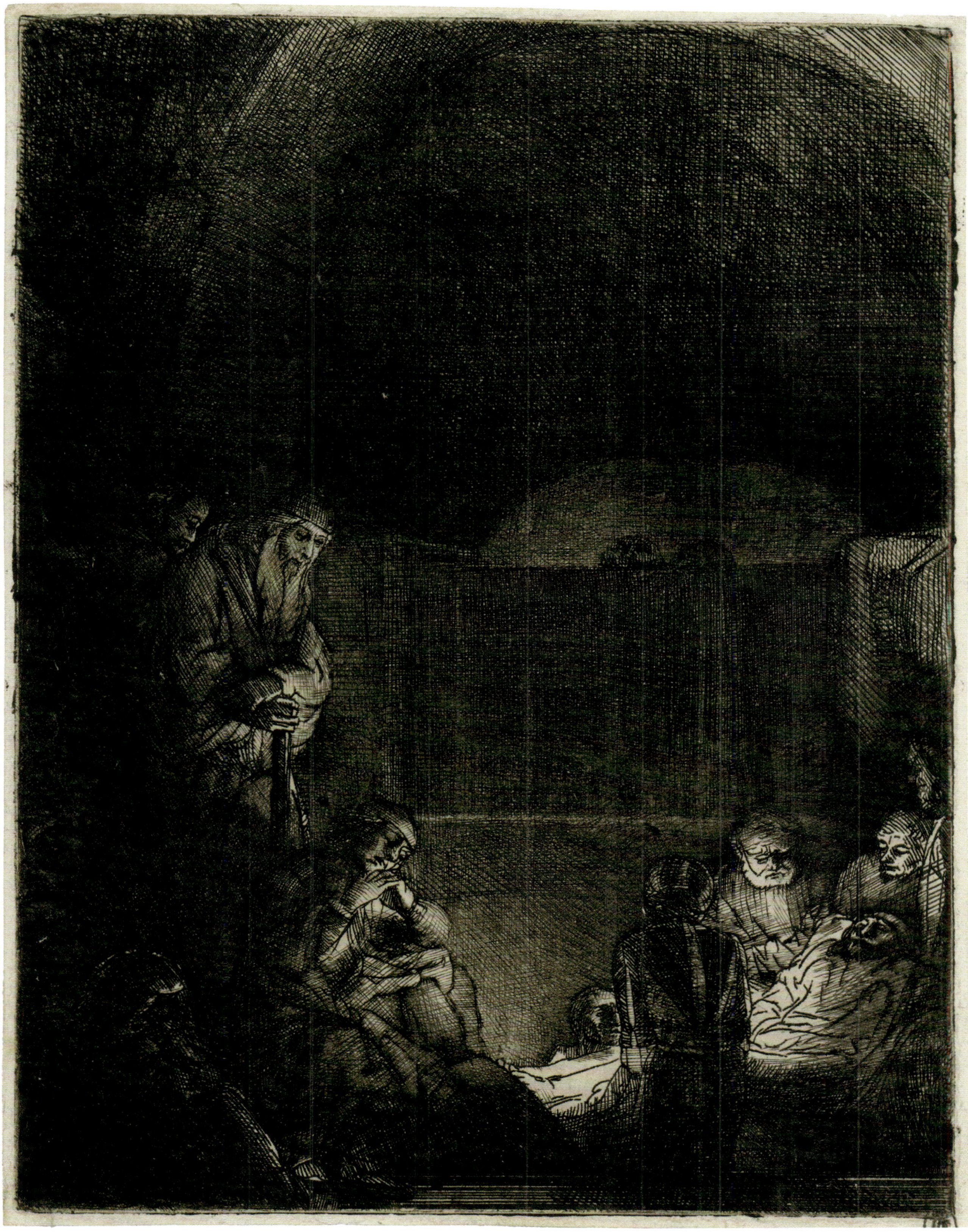

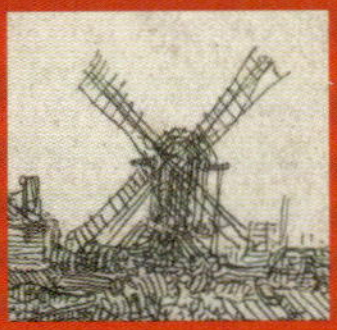

Reflecting nature

In Rembrandt's time landscape prints were enormously popular so it is surprising that he, the consummate businessman, only turned to them between 1640 and 1653 and made no more than twenty-six in total. Most of his landscape prints depict the countryside within a ten-kilometre radius from Amsterdam, south along the river Amstel to Ouderkerk aan de Amstel, or south-east along the Sint Anthonisdijk to Diemen. On the whole he made his earlier landscapes in pure etching and concentrated on their foreground, leaving the background almost entirely blank. His later landscapes made use of drypoint and were more elaborate. At times they also included exotic buildings and mountains which simply did not exist in the environs of Amsterdam.

A common feature of Rembrandt's landscape etchings is their sketchiness. A few meandering lines indicate a tree, and two simple strokes at an angle from a third might signify a sail. A sideways 'v' can be a flag and loosely parallel marks depict water. Rembrandt's mark-making, free, fast and assured at the same time, lends these etchings a rare feeling of spontaneity.

Rembrandt's evocative etched landscapes are miracles of minute observation, repaying close and repeated looking. They focus on everyday and mundane elements such as barns, cottages, barges and windmills. The perfectly placed lines reveal a wealth of detail: figures, animals and domestic architecture, often seen against the Amsterdam skyline.

The intimate, domestic nature of these landscapes has been particularly influential on the work of the Norwich School artists, who depicted the East Anglian landscape – so similar to that of the Netherlands – with a comparable focus on the close observation of nature and attention to the modest and commonplace. In nineteenth-century Norwich Thomas Harvey, patron of Norwich School founder John Crome (1768-1821), owned paintings by Dutch and Flemish Old Masters, including Aelbert Cuyp (1620-1691), Meindert Hobbema (1638-1709) and Jan Steen (1626-1679), as well as prints and drawings by Rembrandt. Crome himself collected Rembrandt's etchings and it was partially Rembrandt's example that led him to focus both on dramatic lighting and on what has been described by Crome's biographers as 'the charm of things scarcely visible'. (Derek and Timothy Clifford, *John Crome*, London: Faber and Faber, 1968, p.57)

View of the Diemerdijk with a Milkman and Cottages ('Het melkboertje')
(III/III), 1650
Etching and drypoint on paper
6.5 x 17.4 cm
NWHCM : 1951.47.56

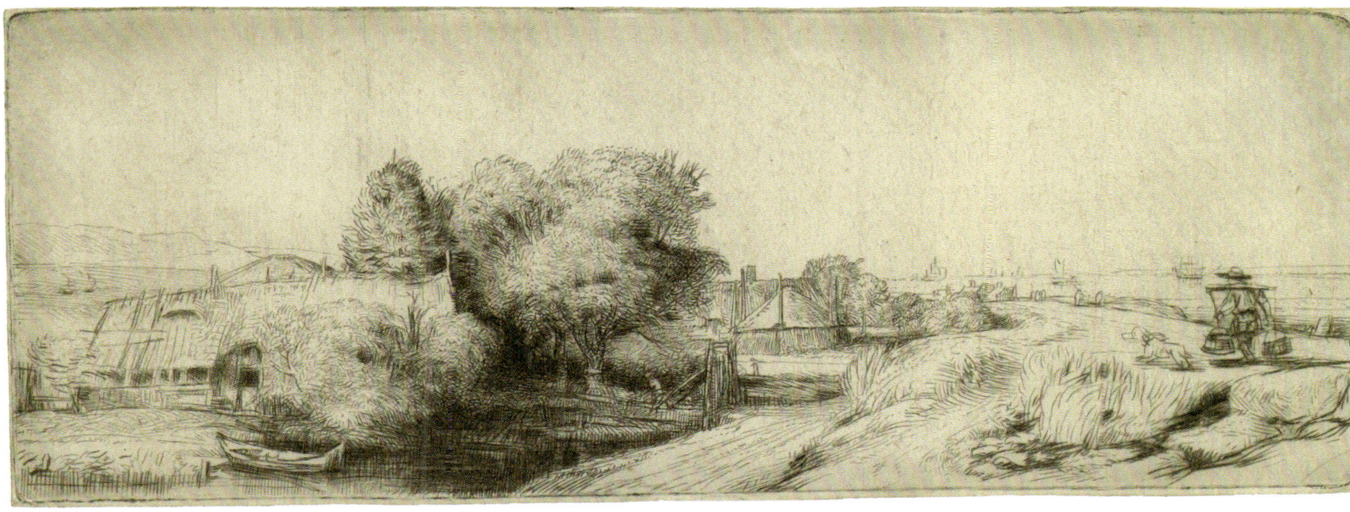

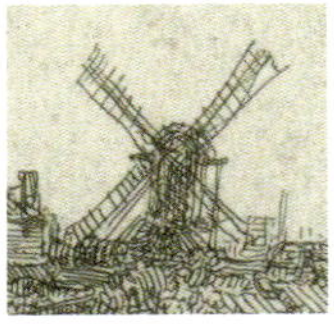

The Windmill (only state), 1641
Etching with touches of drypoint on paper
14.4 x 20.7 cm
Signed and dated in plate lower right corner of subject
'Rembrandt f 1641'
NWHCM : 1951.47.33

Windmills have become synonymous with the Netherlands. In the seventeenth century around nine thousand windmills dotted around the countryside played a significant part in Dutch life. Not only were they used in the timber and paper industries, to grind grains and to make oil but, in a country a quarter of which is below sea level, they were also instrumental in draining the land and preventing floods. One of Rembrandt's most powerful landscape paintings has a windmill as its subject. *The Mill* (c.1645-8, National Gallery of Art, Washington, D.C.) is a dramatic depiction of a lone windmill standing atop a hill overlooking a canal, its sails lit by an unseen sun, black clouds behind it. In 1793 the painting was acquired by Florence Nightingale's grandfather, the MP William Smith from Norwich, who owned it until at least 1815. There is a copy of the painting, known as *The Mill (after Rembrandt van Rijn)*, which has been attributed to John Crome. It is possible that Crome saw Rembrandt's original in Smith's collection or at the British Institution, where it was exhibited twice in Crome's lifetime, in 1806 and 1815.

The windmill depicted by Rembrandt here has been identified with one of the many windmills on the Osdorp rampart near the Lauriergracht canal, south west of Amsterdam. Known as 'de kleine Stinkmolen', or 'the little stink mill', it was used by the tannery industry to soften leather with cod liver oil. This type of multifaceted windmill, which had between six and twelve sides, is known as a 'smock mill'. Rembrandt has dedicated great attention to its component parts. Its sails, mounted on a characteristic rounded cap, are almost hidden to the left. Visible on the right is part of the windmill's tail, an upright post supported by two braces on each side used to turn the windmill's cap with the aid of a capstan wheel. The brake lever, with its long rope hanging down, protrudes beyond. Rembrandt has also depicted a man carrying a heavy sack into the mill and a woman doing her washing in the canal below. The main subject of the windmill and the cottage next to it are depicted in great detail, while the landscape, with two figures in the distance, is barely sketched and the sky is left completely blank. The cracking effect in the sky behind the windmill may have been due to the etching ground cracking when exposed to the acid (Eva Ornstein-Van Slooten and Marijke Holtrop, *The Rembrandt House: a catalogue of Rembrandt etchings*, Zwolle: WBOOKS; Amsterdam: Museum Het Rembrandthuis, 2016, p.127).

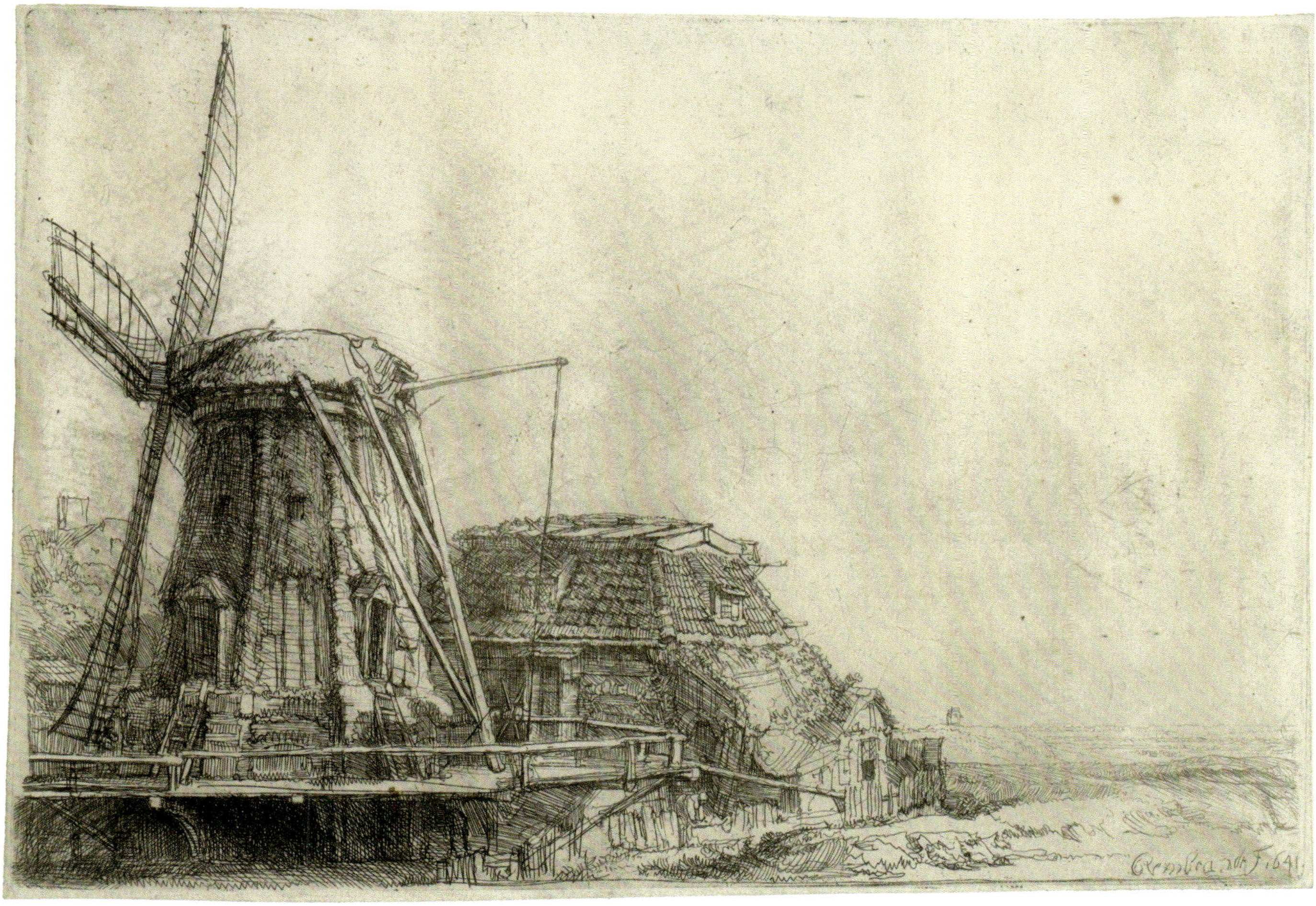

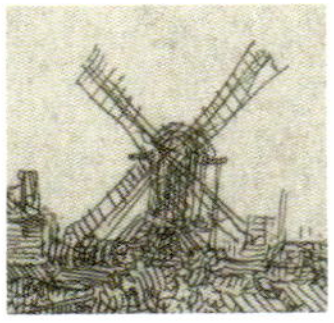

View of Amsterdam from the Kadijk (only state), 1641
Etching on paper
11.3 x 15.4 cm
NWHCM : 1951.47.31

This small but detailed print, just larger than a modern postcard, shows Amsterdam from the north east. It appears to have been taken from the Kadijk, a dike protecting Amsterdam from flooding. It is thought that Rembrandt sketched his design directly on the plate in situ, causing the print to display the view in reverse. In other words, the landmarks visible from left to right were actually right to left in real life, and the IJ bay, seen on the left in the composition, would have been on the right. The scene is depicted from a relatively high vantage point which might indicate that Rembrandt made it from the top of the Kadijk itself.

Several Amsterdam landmarks are recognisable in this print. On the left, the three tallest buildings with spires are, from left to right, the fifteenth-century city defence known as the Herring Packers Tower faintly visible in the far distance, the thirteenth-century Oude Kerk and another city defence known as the Montelban Tower. The large building to the right of the Montelban Tower has been identified as the warehouses of the Dutch East India Company. Next to it is the windmill on the Rijzenhoofd bulwark and, to its right, Rembrandt drew the windmills which rose on Amsterdam's walled fortifications.

In this etching Rembrandt has employed his signature combination of detailed and sketchy mark-making. Although Amsterdam's landmarks are clearly recognisable, the windmills fading into the distance on the right become more and more simplified, and eventually the sails are simply indicated by two crossed lines.

Ships and small groups of people populate the middle ground, while the foreground is entirely taken over by quickly drawn vegetation and a body of water. Rapid strokes are all Rembrandt needed here to give a clear impression of different types of flora, such as grass, bushes and reeds. As with many of his landscape etchings, he has left the sky entirely blank. The low horizon line is typical of seventeenth-century Dutch landscape, and an element which was incorporated by many Norwich School painters in the nineteenth century. Facing each other across the North Sea, the Norfolk and Dutch landscapes are very similar, with big open skies a defining feature of both.

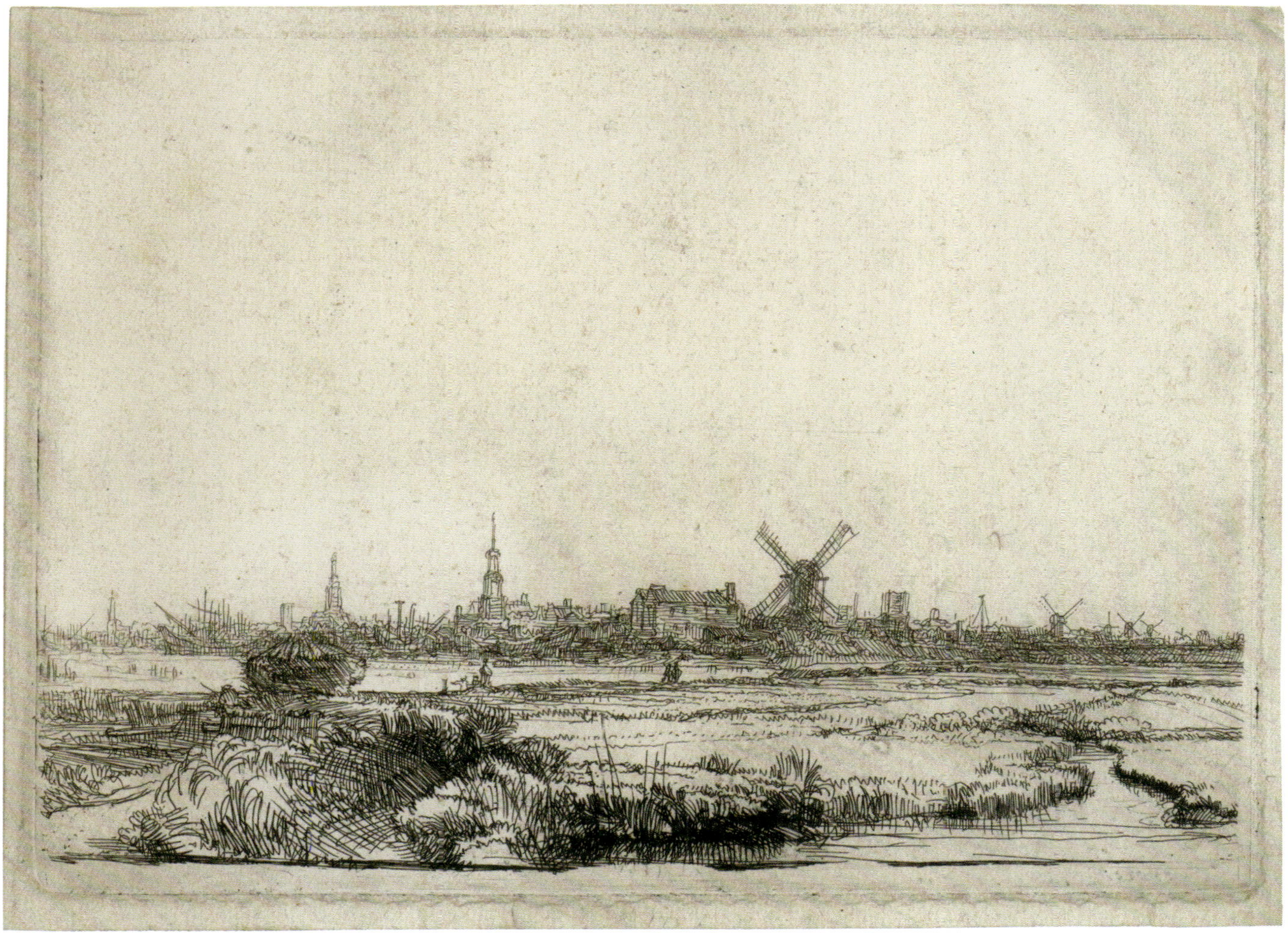

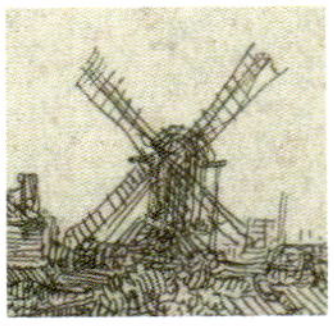

The three Trees (only state), 1643
Etching, engraving and drypoint on paper
21.1 x 28 cm
Signed and dated in plate lower left of subject 'Rembrandt f 1643'
NWHCM : 1951.47.44

The three Trees is Rembrandt's largest and most famous landscape etching. A dark and detailed foreground is subtly backlit by a sky which takes up over half of the composition. Lowering clouds on the edges give way to a clear sky behind the three trees of the title, starkly silhouetting them.

In the foreground Rembrandt has depicted a pool with bushes and reeds growing on its edges. On the left bank there is a man fishing and a woman carrying a basket and wearing a wide-brimmed hat which identify her as a shepherdess. On the right of the foreground a pair of lovers is just visible in the bushes and to their left is a goat, a symbol of sexuality, as if commenting on their behaviour. Receding in the background Rembrandt has depicted other bodies of water and an impressionistic view of Amsterdam on the horizon.

This is a magnificent landscape with a great deal of delightful detail throughout, including different types of bird in the sky. It is also more populated than many other landscapes by Rembrandt. Here he has dotted a variety of people throughout the composition, tending to cattle, sitting on the ground, walking and even travelling in a cart. On the hill to the right Rembrandt has also depicted an artist sketching in the open air. Curiously, the artist is not drawing the landscape that Rembrandt is actually representing, but is looking beyond it to the right instead, capturing another view about which we, the audience, are kept in the dark.

On the left, the cloud section recalls – at a ninety degree angle – that of Rembrandt's *The Death of the Virgin* (see p.26-27). It appears that Rembrandt tried out a first version of *The Death of the Virgin* on this plate then rejected it for a larger one. He then burnished out most of his initial composition while retaining the cloud formation and reusing it for *The three Trees*.

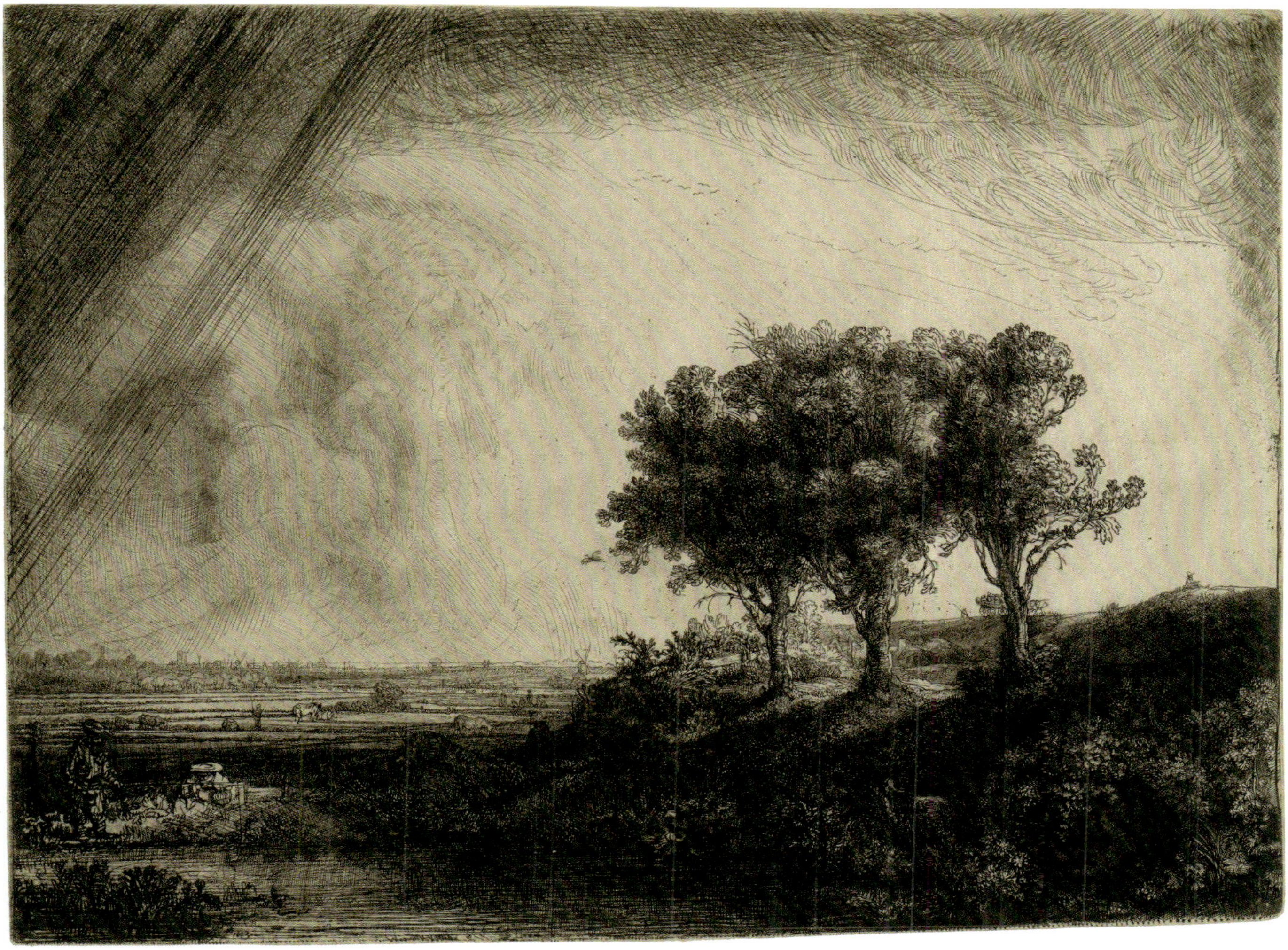

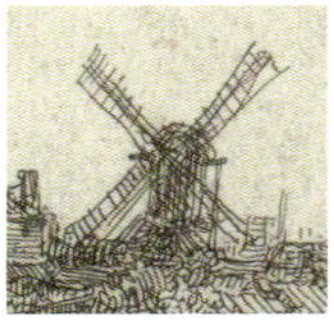

Saint Jerome Reading in an Italian Landscape (II/II), 1653
Etching and drypoint on paper
26 x 20.7 cm
NWHCM : 1951.47.72

Born Eusebius Hyeronimus Sophronius in Dalmatia, Saint Jerome was one of the four Fathers of the Church, a scholar and an ascetic. He was the only Catholic saint that Rembrandt portrayed again and again. Jerome's usual attributes are a cardinal's hat and a lion. The latter refers to Jerome removing a thorn from the foot of an injured lion, who subsequently became his constant companion. In Catholic iconography Saint Jerome was normally depicted as a bearded old man in one of three ways: as a penitent with a skull nearby, beating his chest with a stone; as a learned man in his study surrounded by books and writing materials; as a Doctor of the Church wearing cardinal's robes and often holding a model of a church.

Here Rembrandt has departed from the established depictions of Jerome. He has portrayed the saint very informally, reading in the landscape. The lion is the only indication that Saint Jerome is the subject of the print. The contrast between brightly lit areas and dark shadows point to an idyllic summer's day. Jerome, reading under a tree, is shown wearing a straw hat rather than his usual cardinal's hat and is barefoot, having kicked off his sandals.

The landscape in this print is a radical departure from Rembrandt's usual landscapes. Rather than depicting the country around Amsterdam, it is an imaginary mountainous landscape derived from artistic sources rather than nature. Unlike many of his artistic contemporaries who travelled to Italy to study classical and Renaissance art and architecture, Rembrandt never journeyed abroad or experienced foreign landscapes from life, therefore he based his more exotic views on artistic precedent, drawing particularly from his vast art collection.

In the case of this print, the diagonal structure appears to be derived from the engraving *St Jerome in the Desert* of 1565, made by the Dutch artist Cornelis Cort (c.1533-1578) after a painting by the Venetian master Titian (c.1485/90-1576). Both compositions are dominated on the left by partially bare trees in which a bird is nesting and depict steep mountains on the right hand side. The unusual buildings on the right of Rembrandt's print, however, find their inspiration in another engraving, *St Jerome Reading in a Landscape with a Group of Buildings*, by the Venetian artist Giulio Campagnola (c.1482-1515/18).

In the nineteenth century, this print belonged to King Ferdinand of Portugal (1816-1885). A Prince of Saxe-Coburg and Gotha, Ferdinand became King of Portugal in 1836. He collected Old Master and modern prints. 112 of his Rembrandt prints were included in a sale of his Old Master prints after his death, in November 1893.

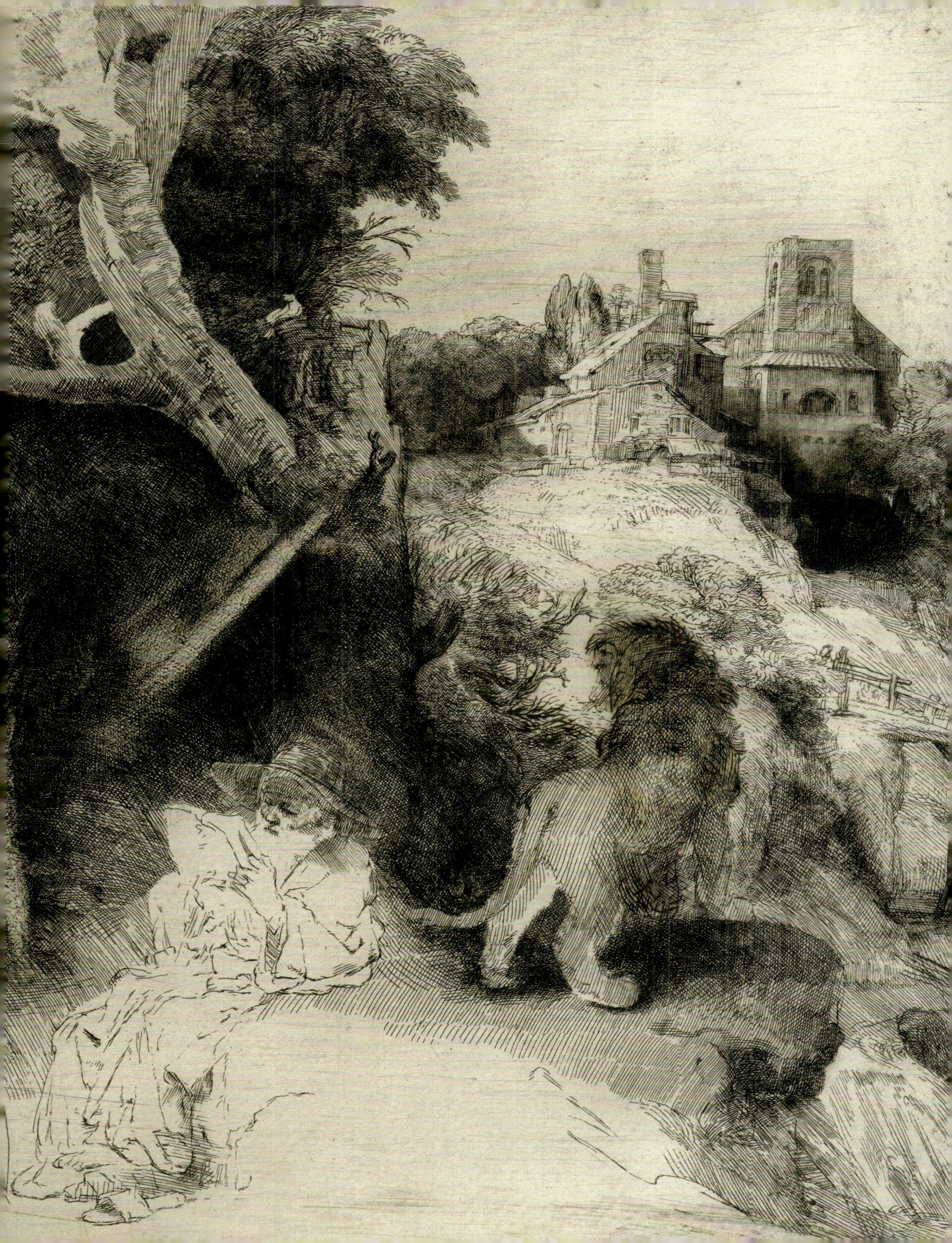

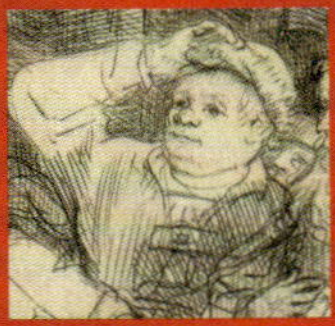

Spotlight on life

Some of Rembrandt's earliest biographers complained that he associated with low company, unsuitable for an esteemed artist who was commissioned by the highest members of society. Rembrandt was ahead of his time in his obvious belief that everything was a suitable subject for art, not just the beautiful, the moral or the ideal. Allied with his interest in personalities and family relationships, he also enjoyed capturing the humdrum details of everyday life: street scenes, people working or at leisure.

Rembrandt etched over fifty vignettes of everyday life, known as 'genre scenes'. Often they portrayed street sellers, musicians, beggars, domestic interiors or workshops. One of his most popular prints during his lifetime was *The Rat Catcher* (also known as *The Rat Poison Pedlar*) from 1632. A somewhat gruesome scene, it shows a rat poison seller at a customer's door. He is holding a pole topped by a cylindrical basket from which dangle a number of rat carcasses, presumably meant to demonstrate the efficacy of his product. A living rat is perched on top of the basket and another is sitting on the man's left shoulder. Rat poison sellers would have been a common sight in Amsterdam in Rembrandt's lifetime, when the plague was a very real and recurring problem.

Often Rembrandt also depicted biblical subjects or scenes from literature as everyday genre scenes, which included contemporary Dutch dress, architecture, interiors or details. This had the effect of rendering them more relatable and realistic, as something that could actually be happening there and then.

Although genre scenes appeared to depict 'real life', they were of course artistic constructs and interpretations. Often artists used them as social commentaries, including moralising or humorous messages. Rembrandt's genre scenes, however, are normally devoid of such messages. Moreover, his subjects are never depicted as ridiculous or grotesque. Whether they are a saint praying or a butcher preparing to slaughter a pig, they are always shown as intrinsically human and equally worthy of our attention.

The Rat Catcher (III/III), 1632
Etching on paper
14 x 12.4 cm
Signed and dated in plate lower right of subject
monogram 'RHL 1632' (the '3' and '2' reversed)
NWHCM : 1951.47.7

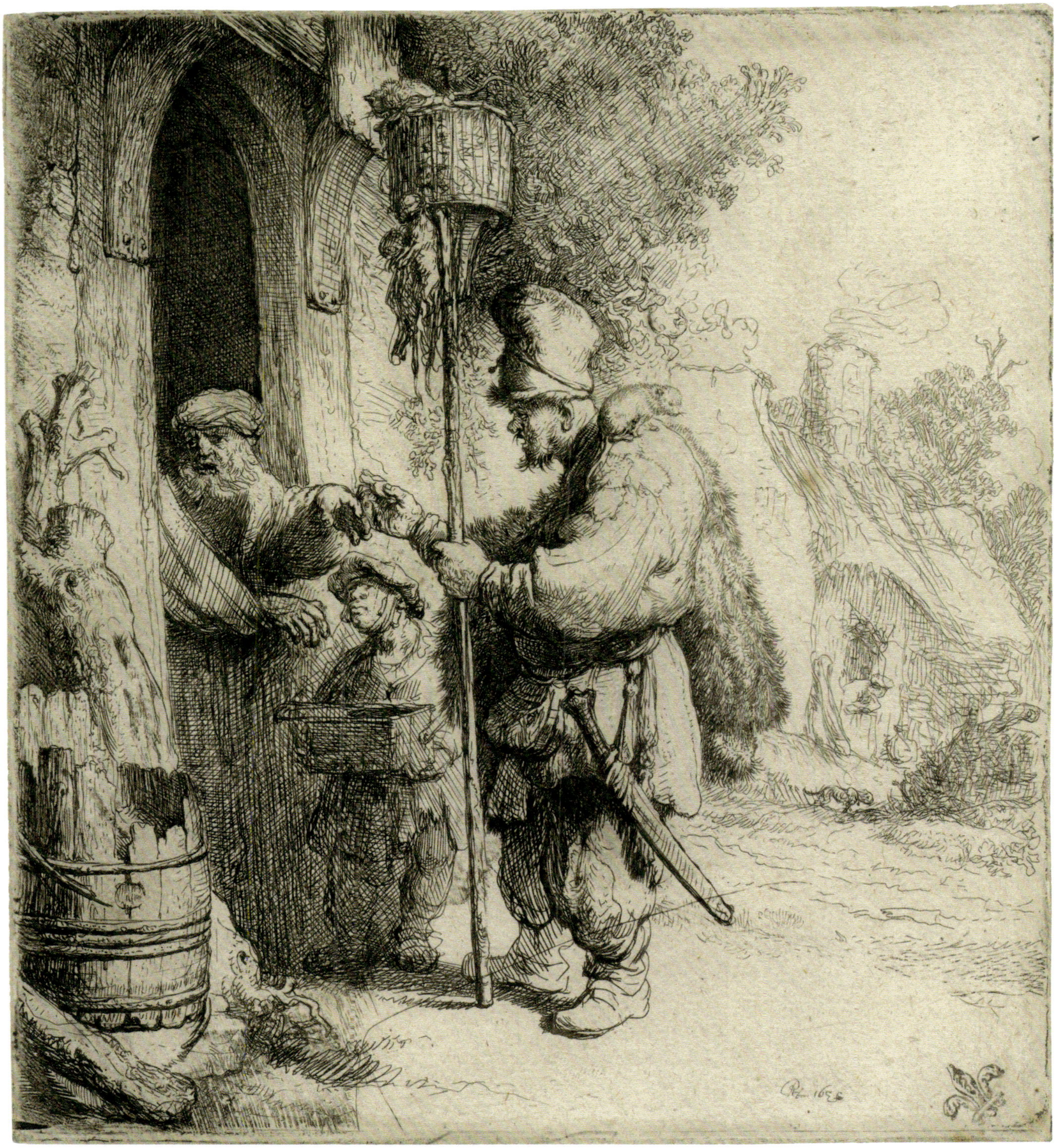

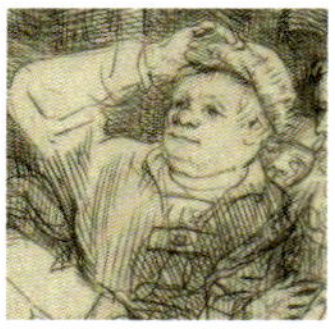

Group of Musicians Listening to a Flute Player, 1635
Brown ink and wash on paper
13.5 x 15.3 cm
NWHCM : 1978.184

Rembrandt made around two thousand drawings of a variety of subjects – historical, biblical, genre, figures, animals, nudes and landscapes. He mainly kept them in albums and it is thought that he often used them as resources on which he and his pupils could draw for inspiration.

This simple drawing in brown ink and wash depicts four musicians in a barely-sketched interior. A flute player sitting on the right is playing his instrument and the other three are listening to him intently. The background is completely blank. Although some parts of the drawing are more detailed, the whole scene exudes freshness and spontaneity, and was clearly drawn very quickly.

Part of what sets Rembrandt apart from a great many artists is his seemingly innate ability to represent something using only the smallest number of lines or the merest touch. This drawing is a wonderful example of this talent. A few thick pen lines are enough to represent an ornate upholstered chair and its shadow. Scant, carefully placed squiggles indicate the flautist's body and hands, though his face and hat are drawn in greater detail. The man to his left is rapidly executed, and Rembrandt only needed a small number of lines to show a clearly rapt expression on his face. Next, standing up, is possibly the most detailed figure, relatively speaking, in the drawing, with luxuriant curls and a thick coat clearly discernible. Finally the man on the far left is the most schematically represented, with the smallest number of thick pen lines indicating his body and face. Indeed, a thick ink comma is all Rembrandt needed here to sketch a closed eye and give the man's face the appearance of concentration.

The drawing is bathed in strong light coming from top left. Rembrandt has successfully conveyed this by carefully placing a few deceptively simple clouds of wash on the lower right of his subjects.

The provenance of this drawing is illustrious and can be traced back to the late eighteenth century, when it was owned by the London banker and Old Master collector Thomas Dimsdale (1758-1823). After his death the drawing was purchased by the Royal painter Sir Thomas Lawrence (1769-1830). Lawrence owned one of the largest and most important collections of prints and drawings of his time. One hundred Rembrandt drawings from his collection – including this one – were sold to William Esdaile (1758-1837), a London banker whose collection of prints and drawings was of the highest order. After Esdaile's death the drawing was sold in the Netherlands, becoming the possession of Baron Jan Gijsbert Verstolk van Soelen (1776-1845), whose collection of Rembrandt prints and drawings is reputed to be one of the best ever known. The drawing was subsequently owned by another Dutch collector, Gerard Leembruggen (1801-1865), who lived in Jan Six's former residence in Hillegom. It was returned to Britain in 1866 when it was purchased by John Malcolm, who also owned our etching *Sheet of Studies with a Woman ill in Bed* (see p.24-25). Captain Geoffrey Malcolm Gathorne-Hardy (1878-1972) later bought this drawing, which stayed in his family by descent until it was allocated to Norwich Castle in lieu of tax in 1978.

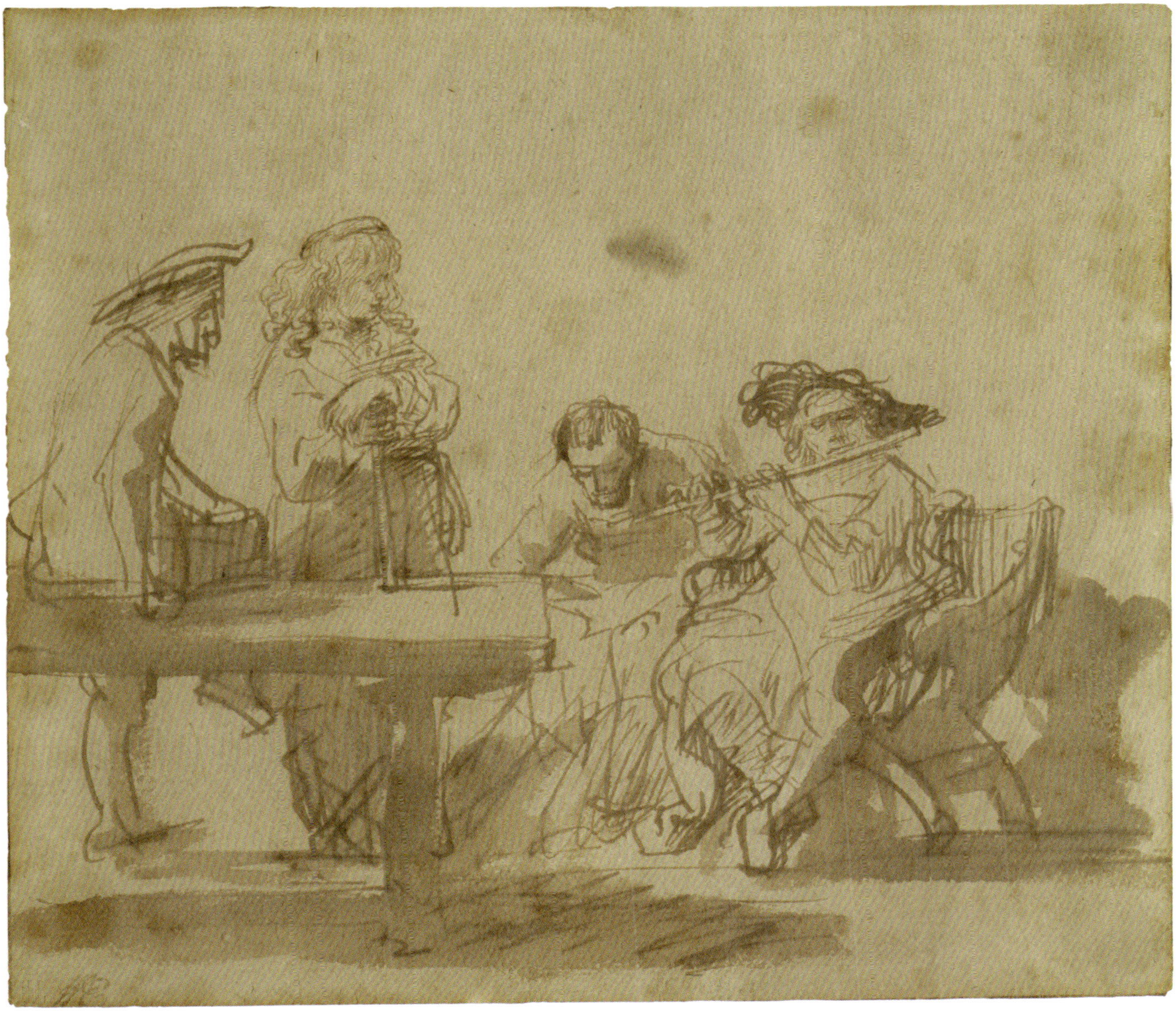

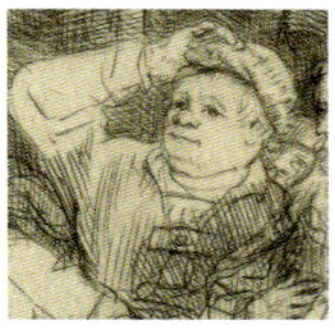

The Pancake Woman (II/VII), 1635
Etching on paper
10.9 x 7.9 cm
Signed and dated in plate lower centre of subject
'Rembrandt. Ft 1635'
NWHCM : 1951.47.14

The motif of the pancake seller dates from the mid-sixteenth century and was popular in Rembrandt's time. Traditionally it was associated with depictions of Shrove Tuesday, but by the seventeenth century it had become a genre subject in its own right.

Although this print is extremely small, Rembrandt has managed to incorporate an astonishing amount of detail in a tiny space. Central to the scene is the pancake seller, dressed in black and concentrating intently on the pancakes cooking in front of her. She is surrounded by a crowd, mostly children, in a variety of poses. On the left of the scene a smiling toddler, straining to watch the pancake seller at work, is held up by a woman. Behind them two boys, one holding up a coin, are waiting for their turn, grinning in anticipation. To their right another boy is bending down, watching the pancake seller. The face of the child next to him has broken into an expression of sheer joy after biting into a freshly-cooked pancake; his coat may be patched at the elbow, but in this moment of happiness poverty can be momentarily forgotten. A small child to the far right is watching the cooking process with an air of longing.

Rembrandt has included a humorous vignette right at the front of his composition. A small, determined dog is attempting to steal a pancake from a little boy who twists away from him with a suitably outraged look on his face. Hidden in the shadows to their right a cat looks on, perhaps hoping for the scraps that might result from the tussle or for a pancake to fall from the skillet. The boy's twisting pose derives from a *putto* in the foreground of Raphael's fresco *The Triumph of Galatea*, c.1514, although, characteristically, Rembrandt turned the poised, classicising *putto* into an angry street urchin. The fresco was known from engravings by several artists, including the leading Dutch engraver Hendrick Goltzius (1558-1617). Rembrandt owned a book of prints by Goltzius as well as four books of prints by or after Raphael.

This impression is the second state of seven and the last one entirely in Rembrandt's hand.

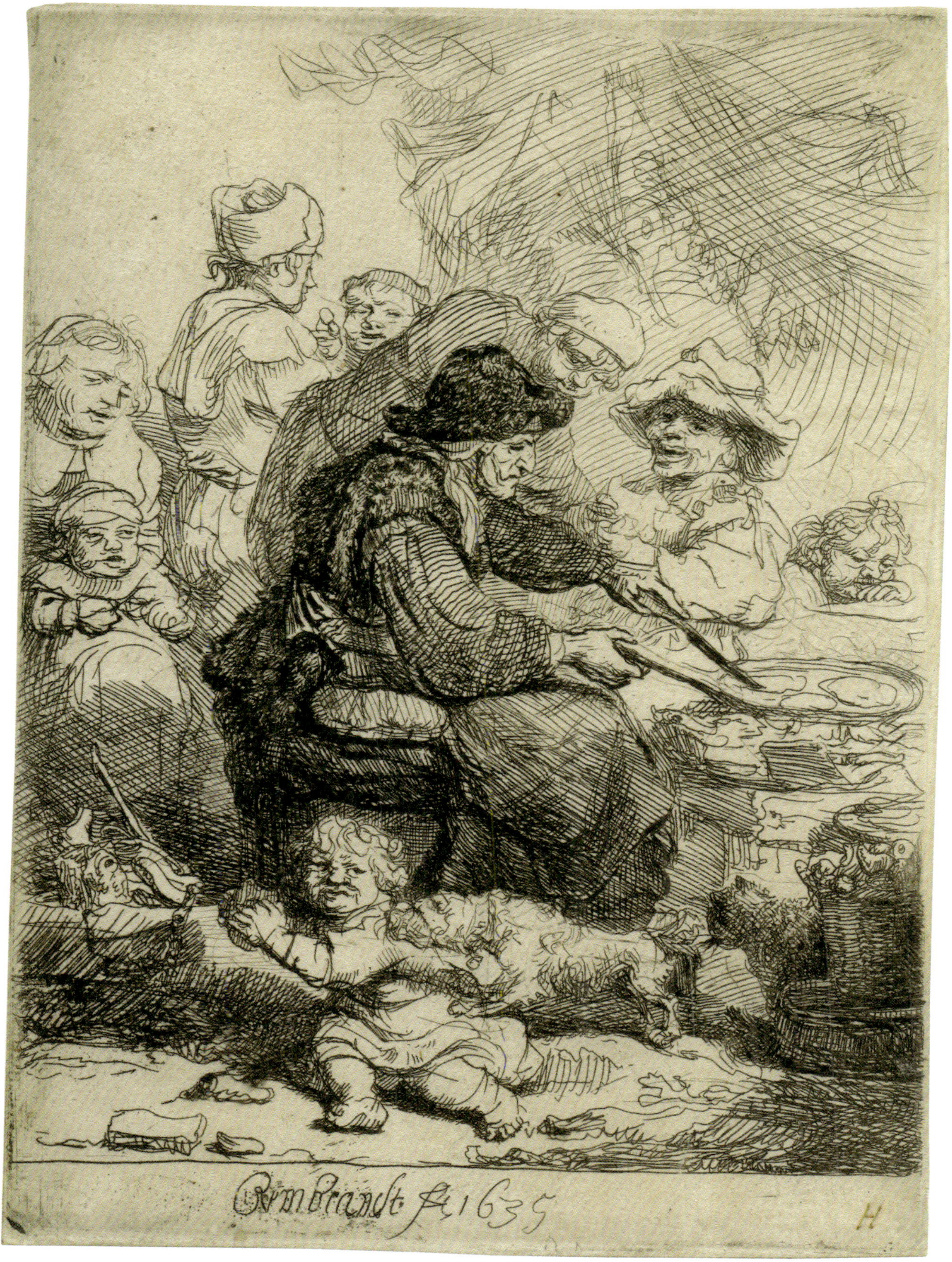
Rembrandt f. 1635
H

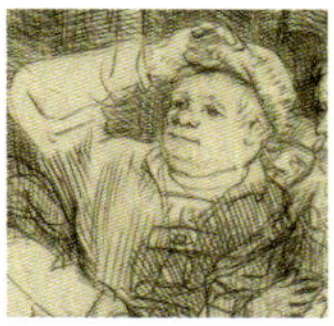

The Triumph of Mordecai (III/IV), 1641
Etching and drypoint on paper
17.3 x 21.3 cm
NWHCM : 1951.47.36

Mordecai is one of the main protagonists of the Book of Esther in the Hebrew Bible. A minister at the Persian King Ahasuerus' court, he foiled a plot to murder the king. Some time later, wishing to reward Mordecai, the king asked his grand vizier Haman what he should do 'for the man the king delights to honour'. Haman, thinking the king referred to him, answered "have them bring a royal robe the king has worn and a horse the king has ridden ... Then let the robe and horse be entrusted to one of the king's most noble princes. Let them robe the man ... and lead him on the horse through the city streets, proclaiming before him, 'This is what is done for the man the king delights to honour!'" (Esther 6:6-9) Ahasuerus then commanded Haman to lead Mordecai in triumph through the streets of Susa, unaware that Haman had been working to bring about the annihilation of all Persian Jews through his hatred of Mordecai. Through Queen Esther, Mordecai's niece, Ahasuerus later discovered Haman's deceit and had him impaled outside his home.

Rembrandt's etching depicts the moment that Haman, who was indeed 'one of the king's most noble princes', is made to lead Mordecai in triumph through the city wearing a rich fur-trimmed cloak. King Ahasuerus and Queen Esther are watching from a balcony and a great crowd has assembled along the street: rich and poor, old and young, including a baby in its mother's arms who is wearing a type of skullcap that often features in Rembrandt's prints. Some people are kneeling or even prostrating themselves before Mordecai. Rembrandt has created a tense atmosphere: soldiers follow carrying spears and a guard is preparing to strike a bystander; two dogs to the right are barking furiously. Mordecai's face is full of gravitas while Haman's expresses worry. By this time he has realised that this is the beginning of his downfall.

The right side of the print is somewhat sketchy, bathed in light and rendered almost entirely in etching, while Rembrandt used drypoint extensively on the darker left side. Rembrandt used two notable depictions of *The Triumph of Mordecai* as sources for this composition, a 1515 engraving by Lucas van Leyden (1494-1533) and a painting by his former teacher Pieter Lastman (1583–1633) dated 1617. In particular from van Leyden he borrowed the man kneeling to the right and the one removing his hat behind him, while Lastman's painting also included a gateway and people watching from a high balcony.

Rembrandt returned to the Book of Esther several times in his life; the themes clearly appealed to him. As early as 1635 he started the painting *Haman Begging the Mercy of Esther*, which is thought to have been almost completely repainted in his workshop in the 1660s (National Museum of Art of Romania, Bucharest). In later life he painted *Ahasuerus and Haman at the Feast of Esther*, 1660 (Pushkin Museum, Moscow) and *Haman Prepares to Honour Mordecai,* c.1665 (Hermitage Museum, St Petersburg).

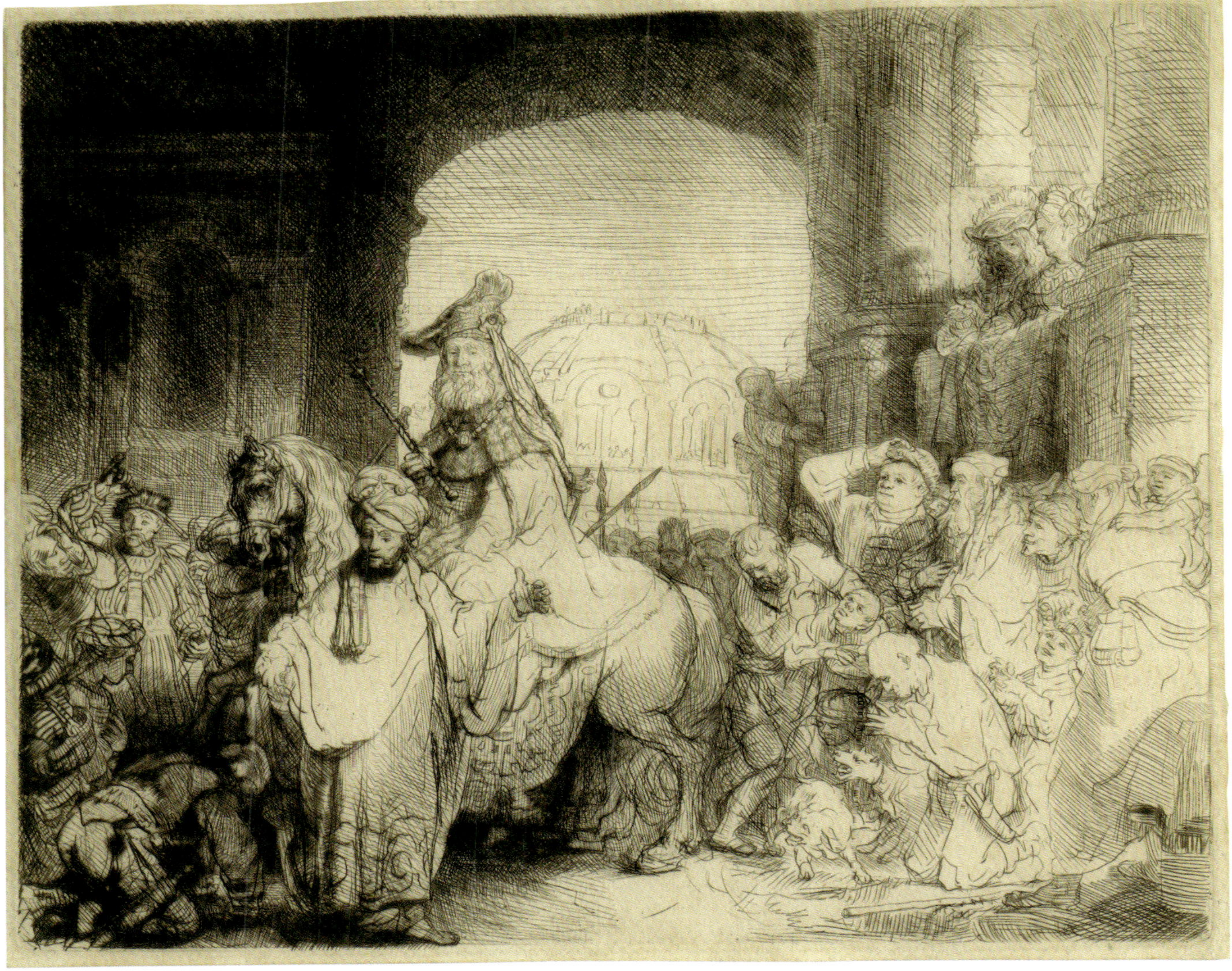

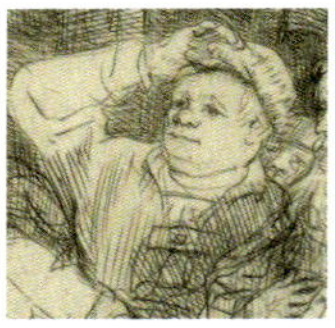

The Hog (II/II), 1643
Etching and drypoint on paper
14.3 x 15.4 cm
Signed and dated in plate lower right of subject 'Rembrandt f / 1643'
NWHCM : 1951.47.40

This etching depicts a sow lying on the ground waiting to be slaughtered; her trotters are tied together with a rope which is tethered to a post nearby. In spite of her predicament she appears calm, almost relaxed. Behind her a laughing boy holds an inflated pig's bladder. A curious toddler, supported by a woman and wearing the skullcap typical of many Rembrandt compositions, is observing the scene. A doorway shows an interior in the background, where a man with a full moustache is sharpening an axe. Almost invisible, the axe is barely indicated by half a dozen fine lines.

The slaughter of large animals in Rembrandt's time traditionally took place towards the end of the year, in November. In art, slaughter scenes found their origins in the medieval cycles known as 'Labours of the Months', which associated rural activities including sowing, ploughing, harvesting and animal slaughter with different months of the year. By the seventeenth century, however, they had become popular genre scenes in their own right and Rembrandt famously depicted a visceral *Slaughtered Ox* in 1655 (Musée du Louvre, Paris).

Here Rembrandt has slightly departed from tradition as he is depicting the moment before the slaughter, rather than the slaughter itself. He has, however, included the traditional element of laughing children, as well as an inflated pig's bladder. This was an 'exceptionally popular motif' in Dutch painting, especially in slaughter scenes. It was found in contemporary emblem books as 'a symbol of earthly transience'. (Holm Bevers, Peter Schatborn and Barbara Welzel, *Rembrandt: the Master & his Workshop: Drawings & Etchings*, New Haven and London: Yale University Press; London: National Gallery Publications, 1991, p.216)

Soap bubbles and inflated animal bladders in art were well-known *vanitas* elements. Both were associated with the concept of *homo bulla* ('man is a bubble'), which compared human life to the fragility of a soap bubble. Originating in Roman times, the idea was revived in the sixteenth century by Erasmus of Rotterdam (1469-1536) who wrote, 'Man is but a bubble. The lesson of this proverb is that there is nothing so fragile, so fleeting and so empty as the life of man. A bubble is that round swollen empty thing which we watch in water as it grows and vanishes in a moment of time.' (William Barker, *The Adages of Erasmus*, Toronto: University of Toronto Press, 2001, p.171)

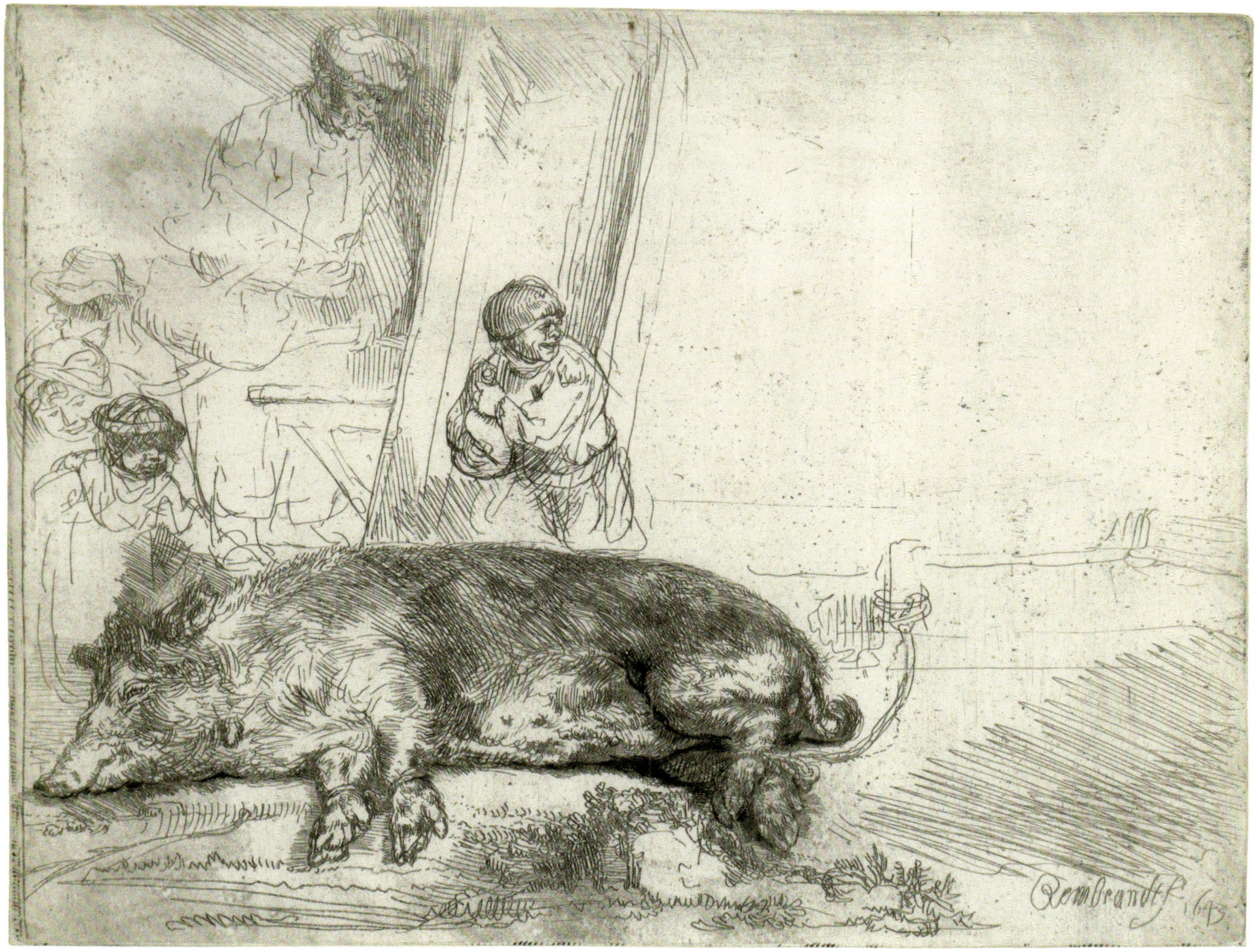
Rembrandt f. 1643

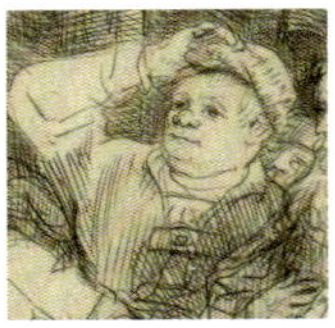

A blind Hurdy-gurdy Player and Family Receiving Alms
(I/V), 1648
Etching and drypoint on paper
16.4 x 12.8 cm
Signed and dated in plate lower right of subject
'Rembrandt f. 1648'
NWHCM : 1951.47.49

Rembrandt had an interest in all levels of society and in his early life he portrayed himself as a beggar as well as a gentleman. Many of his scenes of everyday life reflect his interest in depicting characters like vagrants, street sellers and strolling musicians.

Here he has depicted a hurdy-gurdy player with his young family at the door of a prosperous-looking house. The hurdy-gurdy, here in shadow and partially obscured, is a stringed instrument played by turning a crank; historically it was often played by blind itinerant musicians. The musician depicted here by Rembrandt is also blind.

Some features of this etching are familiar from other subjects of Rembrandt's. Most clearly, the musician, with his unseeing eyes, prominent features and wispy white beard, recalls Rembrandt's most famous etched blind subject, Tobit (see p.40-41). The headgear worn by all the different characters can also be spotted in other etchings.

While Rembrandt left an empty area to the right of the etching, the scene is full of interesting detail. The house's architecture, with a covered gutter running in front of the doorway, is indicated in just enough detail to hint at its grandeur. Similarly, the clothes of the man in the doorway, who is handing out a coin with a kindly expression on his lined face, indicate his wealth. Ragged clothes, sandals and various items hanging from belts all point to the musician's family being in need, and yet these details are drawn without an implied comment about the disparity in status between them and the man giving them charity. From Rembrandt they all receive the same amount of attention and consideration.

Only this, the first state of this subject, is entirely in Rembrandt's hand; the next four were altered after his death.

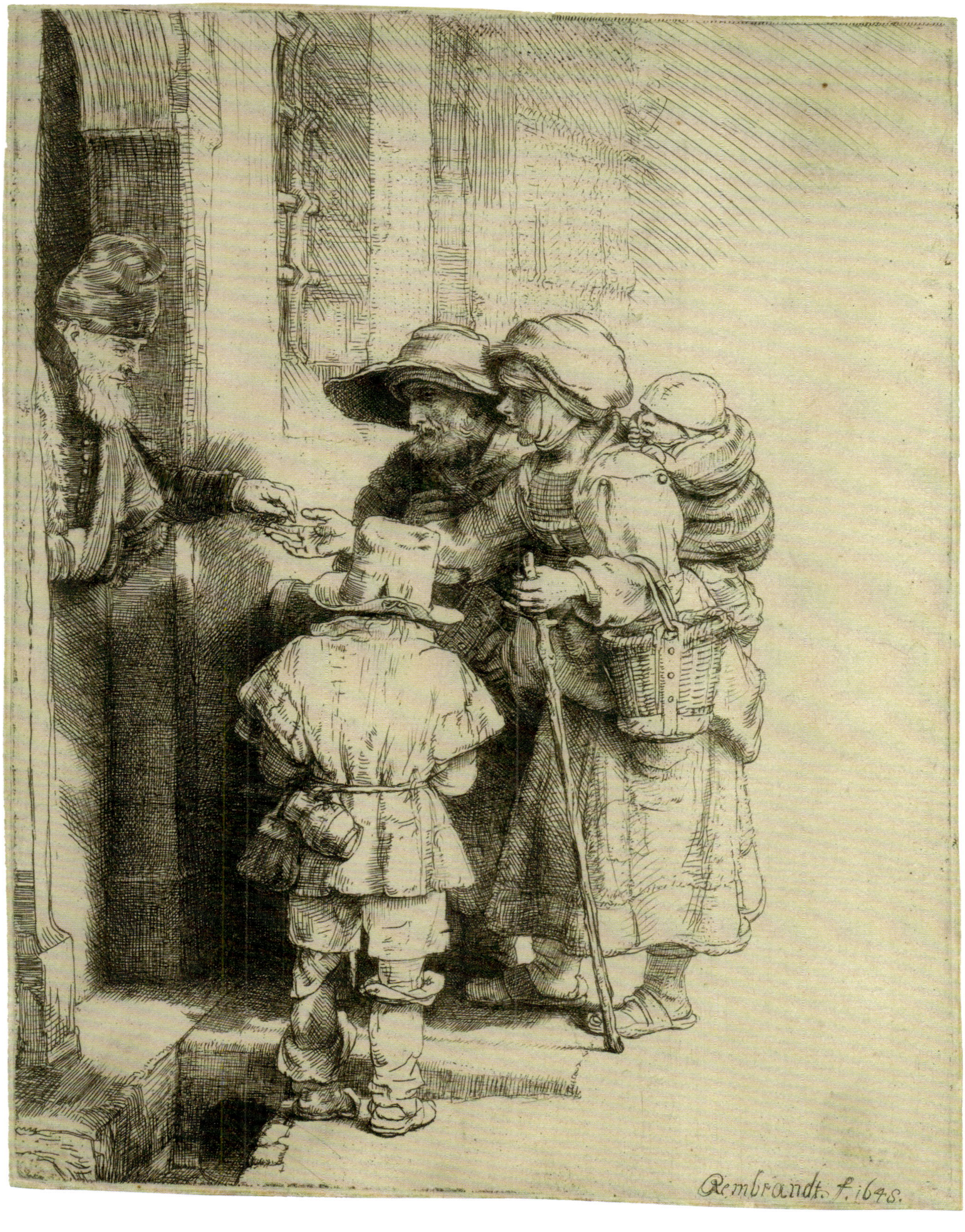
Rembrandt. f. 1648.

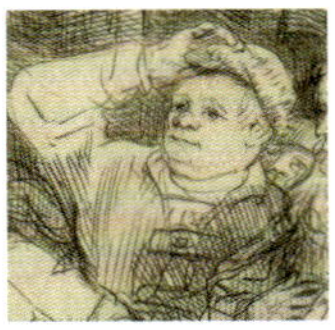

A Scholar in his Study ('Faust') (I/VIII), 1652
Etching, engraving and drypoint on oatmeal paper
21 x 16.1 cm
NWHCM : 1951.47.70

This print is highly unusual, as unlike all Rembrandt's other subjects it depicts a supernatural scene. Visually it bears some relation to his painting *Belshazzar's Feast* (c.1636, National Gallery, London) illustrating the Old Testament story of the blasphemous king Belshazzar's banquet, during which a divine hand appears, writing words which prophesy his doom.

This print, however, is not biblical, and the scene is portrayed in a realistic seventeenth-century interior. A man is in his study, among his papers, a globe by his side. As he turns to the window, the source of natural light, a shadowy figure reveals itself. Only its hands are fully visible, which point towards a mirror. A glowing disc, inscribed with strange words, conceals the figure's face.

As the traditional subtitle to this print implies, it has been thought that the scholar represents Faust, who sold his soul to the Devil in return for knowledge. This literary character was known in Rembrandt's Amsterdam, but the first known identification of this scholar with Faust does not occur until the mid-eighteenth century, so cannot be considered conclusive.

What does seem clear is that Rembrandt is portraying an aspect of one of his central themes: that of a moment of enlightenment and revelation, even though in this case we do not understand its nature. The inscription, written in circular format, containing apparently meaningless words, resembles the type of Cabbalistic incantation frequently illustrated in early modern magical works, such as the Renaissance *Key of Solomon*. This inscription has not been deciphered however, and the only clearly intelligible word is at the centre of the disc. 'INRI' is the standard abbreviation for *Iesus Nazarenus Rex Iudeorum*, 'Jesus of Nazareth, King of the Jews', which was written above Jesus' cross.

These letters, plus the presence of the mirror, have led to interpretations of this scene as a moral lesson on the nature of human knowledge. The mirror is a divine reminder that in this world humanity only sees 'as through a glass darkly', as St Paul wrote in his first letter to the Corinthians (I Corinthians 13, v. 12). In this world perfect knowledge is not possible through human striving. Only in the next world is this achievable, through a focus on God, the true source of wisdom.

The other, related possibility is that the mysterious figure gestures towards the mirror to show the scholar clearly to himself, humbling him by revealing his humanity and imperfection. Of this the skull, traditional symbol of mortality, may also serve as a reminder. The disc may indeed portray some arcane wisdom magically revealed through the scholar's learning, but the name of Jesus remains at its centre. Contemporary magical, scientific and alchemical literature repeatedly reminded such seekers after knowledge that their work should be undertaken in a spirit of reverence and piety, to avoid the dangers of either black magic or hubristic arrogance. Rembrandt may be illustrating a double-edged moment of enlightenment for this scholar in his dark study: that of understanding a secret which had been hidden from him, and at the same time showing his need, as a mere mortal, to keep God at the centre of his life.

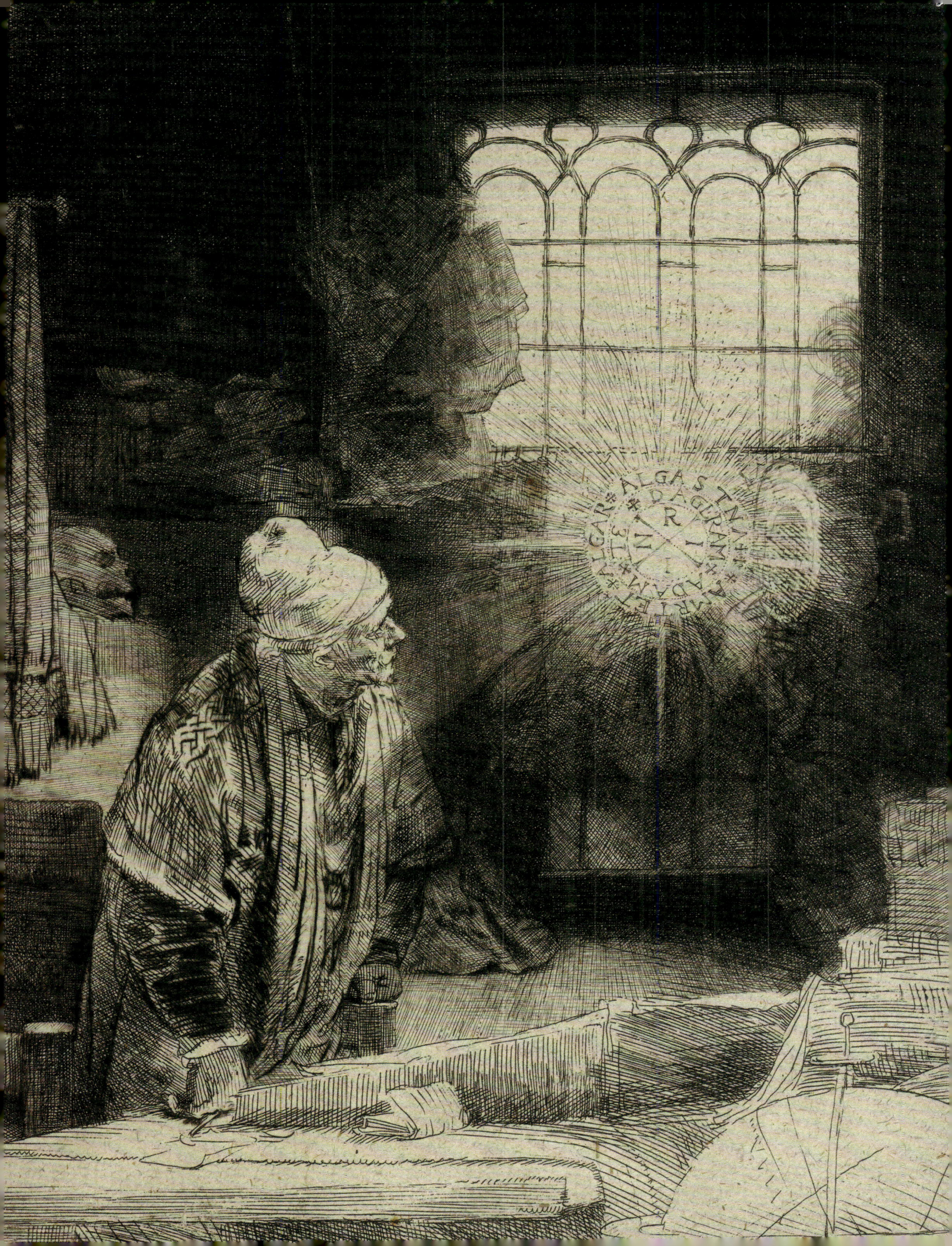

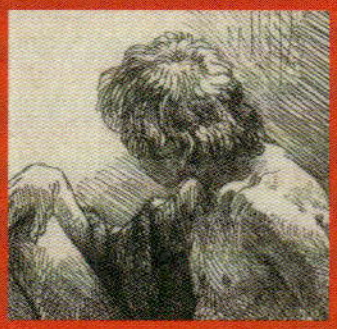

Revealing the body

Comparatively few of Rembrandt's works feature nude figures, but nonetheless they were startling in his time and may still surprise us today. For much of his career he taught students at his home and employed life models frequently. Surviving drawings depict models sitting in a high-windowed space which is easily recognisable as Rembrandt's studio, still existing in what is now the Rembrandt House Museum in central Amsterdam.

Rembrandt's approach to the body shocked his contemporaries because, rather than depicting the more idealised classically beautiful figures fashionable at the time, he focused on bodies as they really were. This attitude was frequently misunderstood and criticised. Many people complained that his figures, especially his women, were far too ugly to be appropriate subjects for art.

However, although curves, wrinkles, dimples and lumps are depicted uncompromisingly, Rembrandt's subjects are never portrayed in a demeaning or grotesque way. Indeed, imperfections seem to be what makes them human and interesting. In subsequent centuries this realism excited and inspired other artists. Among the first were Edouard Manet (1832-1883) and Edgar Degas (1834-1917), who caused scandal among their own contemporaries in nineteenth-century France, drawing on Rembrandt's example in their desire to depict real people in modern society.

Woman Bathing her Feet at a Brook (I/II), 1658
Etching and drypoint on paper
15.9 x 8 cm
Signed and dated in plate 'Rembrandt / f. 1658'
NWHCM : 1951.47.91

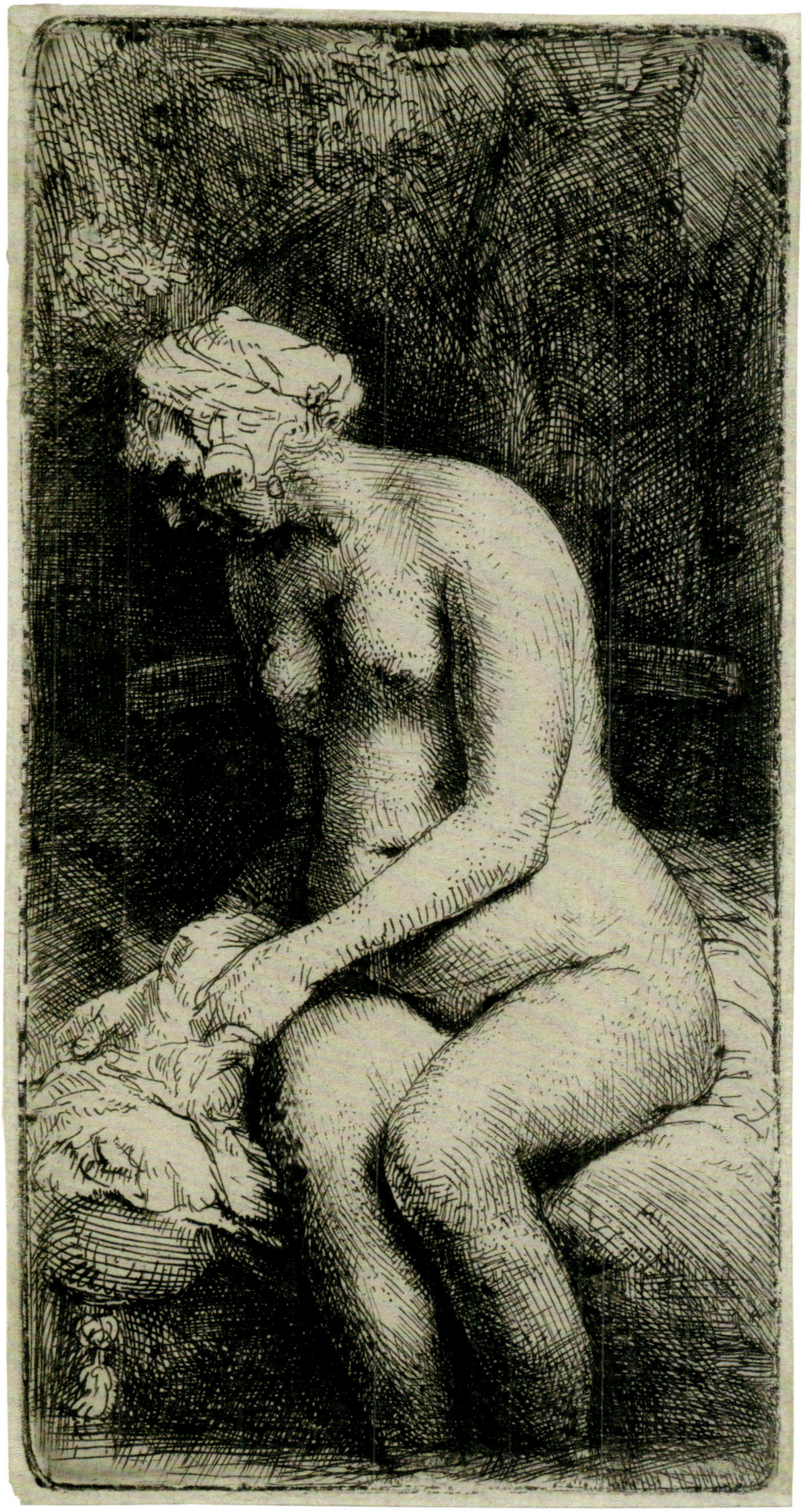

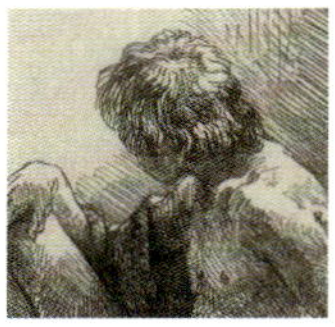

Naked Woman Seated on a Mound (II/II), 1631
Etching and engraving on paper
17.7 x 16.1 cm
Signed in plate upper left barely visible monogram 'RHL'
NWHCM : 1951.47.5

Rembrandt's approach to the human body was as revolutionary as his approach to printmaking. This engaging nude study epitomises his directness and realism and, as such, has come in for particularly harsh criticism. The model's soft flesh includes abundant curves and bulges, the stretchmarks on her rotund stomach suggesting she has borne children. The identity of this model is unknown. It has been thought that she resembles Saskia but it is not known if Rembrandt had met his future wife as early as 1631, and even if he had, she would have been highly unlikely to have posed nude for him. The woman depicted here also appears older than Saskia, who would have been no more than nineteen at this date.

The model closely resembles the female nude figure in another print made in the same year, *Diana at the Bath* (for an example see the British Museum's version). As Diana, the model's hair is bound rather than flowing loose, and her pose has been twisted round to provide a side-view, with a more clearly emphasised woodland background. Rembrandt may have worked on these prints alongside each other following a sitting with the life model, perhaps deciding between two poses as to which was best suited to represent the mythological scene of the goddess Diana bathing. He may have intended to incorporate the pose seen here into an accompanying composition from the familiar classical tale, perhaps depicting one of Diana's companions, such as the nymph Callisto.

For the second state, Rembrandt re-worked the plate, changing the lighting to allow more dramatic shadows to fall on the side of the model's face and her right shoulder, and adding highlights to her stomach, thigh and right foot. For Rembrandt the printing plate was an ever-changing means of experimentation. Many distinguished previous artists had portrayed the goddess Diana and her nymphs, but none had portrayed such a realistic and un-idealised female body, goddess or mortal.

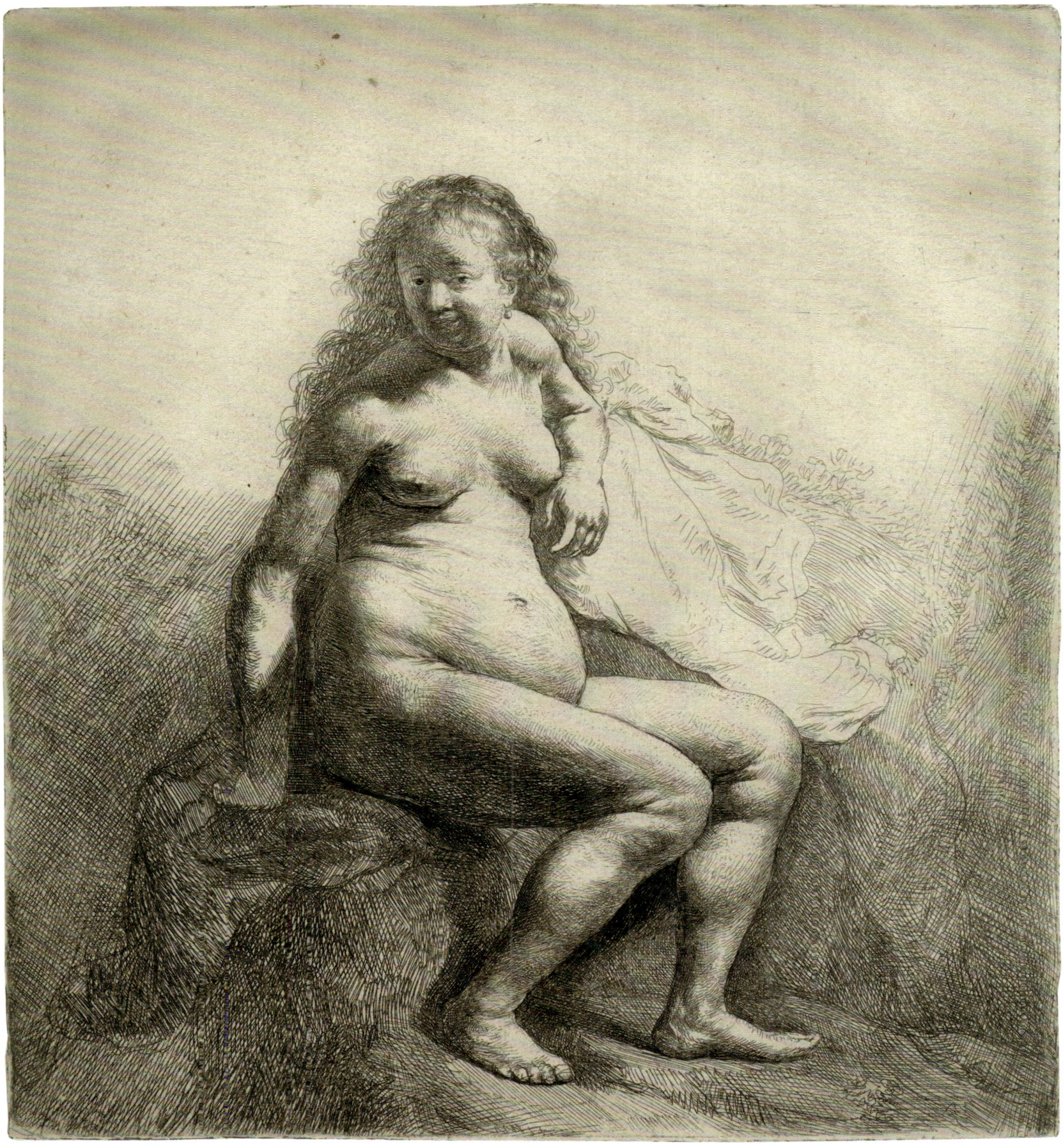

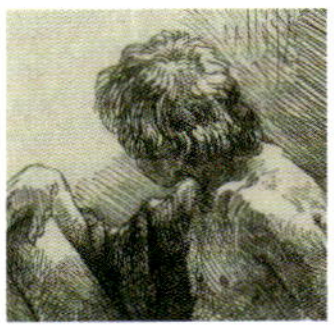

The Crucifixion, small Plate (I/III), 1635
Etching on paper
9.5 x 6.7 cm
Signed in plate upper centre 'Rembrandt f.'
NWHCM : 1951.47.15

Rembrandt was to complete several versions of the Crucifixion over the course of his life, giving him the opportunity to explore many aspects of this most heart-rending, centrally important Christian subject. This relatively early version is executed in etching only.

This version was undertaken following Rembrandt's series of five paintings on aspects of Christ's Passion commissioned in 1632. It differs from his interpretation of the Crucifixion for this series however, by his choice of placing the Cross to one side. This is relatively unusual for portrayals of the Crucifixion. In most artists' work Jesus is usually placed frontally at the centre, the chief focus for the devotion of the viewer, together with the mourners, Mary, St John, Mary Magdalen and others below him, sometimes flanked by the two thieves on their crosses, on either side. The view Rembrandt chooses here places equal emphasis on both Jesus and the group of mourners. The angles of the figures and the placing of the Cross make the picture visually complex and interesting, and allow Rembrandt scope to exhibit his technical skill, portraying the scene at an oblique angle.

This grouping of Cross and people creates a diagonal composition, the figures and their activity balanced by a large area of empty white space to the upper right. Against this white space, even though placed to one side, Jesus still stands out clearly. His face is shadowed, but his body is depicted realistically with no attempt at idealisation. He is thin and slumped, the effects of gravity visible in the slight bulge of his belly over his loincloth. The other figures too are real: an unglamorous-looking Mary Magdalen crouches beneath the Cross, the Virgin is limp and crumpled in grief, the standing man to the right is raising his hands in prayer, the gesture intensified by his anguished face. So much of the success of Rembrandt's work depends on his portrayals of real human beings in everyday situations, whether capturing the face, the body or both. A work like this would have been built up from many studies from life, until he had captured the essence of each pose, how each figure, their facial expressions and the positions of their bodies could combine together to contribute to the overall meaning of the composition.

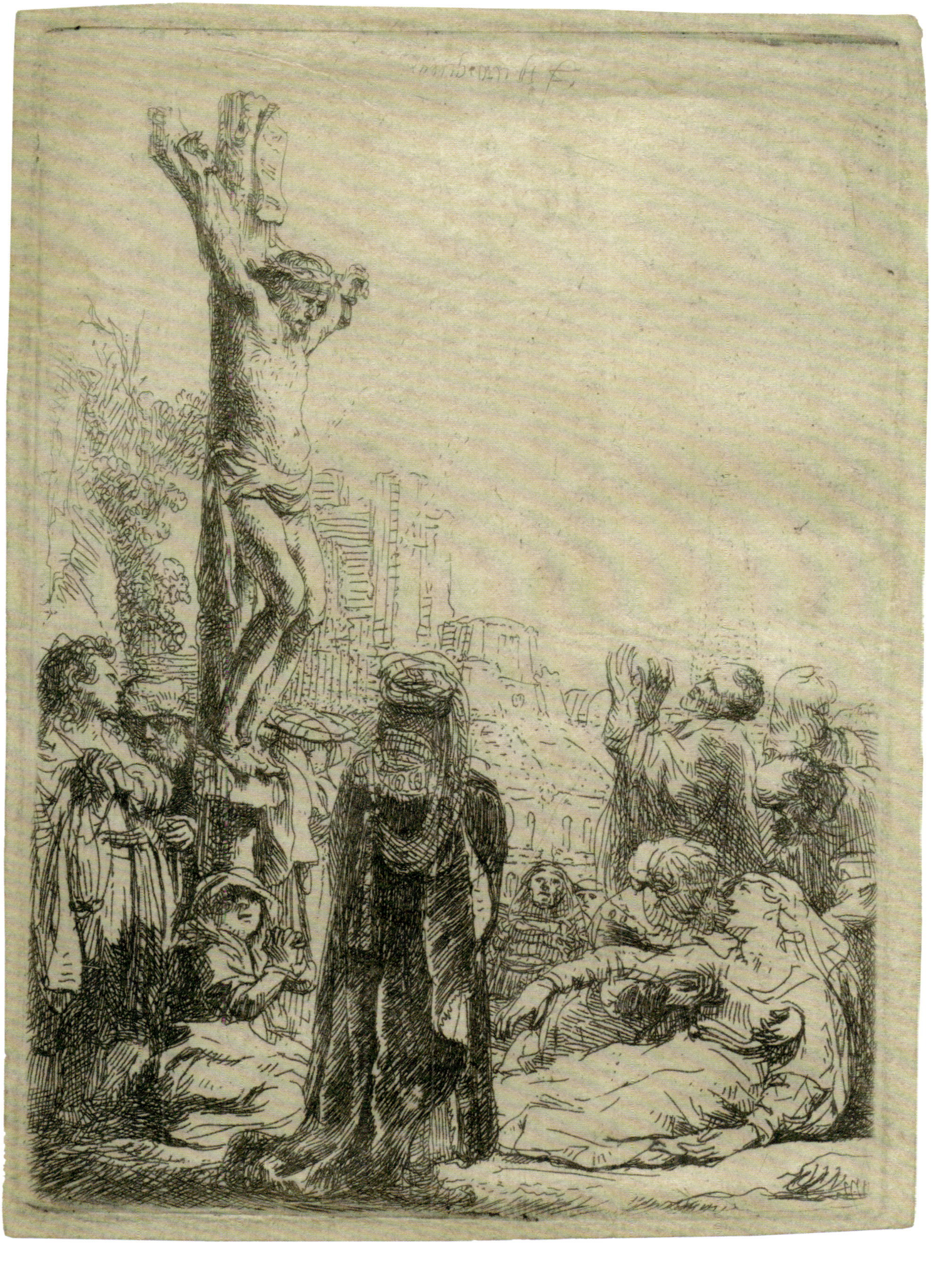

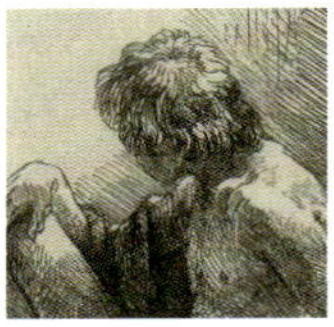

Nude – Man Seated on the Ground with one Leg Extended
(II/III), 1646
Etching and engraving on paper
9.7 x 16.6 cm
Signed and dated in plate lower left of subject
'Rembrandt. f. 1646'
NWHCM : 1951.47.47

Rembrandt's nude studies in print form can be grouped by date. His few prints featuring the male nude were dated 1646. They were probably all sketched from the same model and could have been etched onto the plate directly during the modelling session, without the intermediary stage of a drawing. This study, like the plump female nude of 1631 on p.84-85, has been criticised periodically over the centuries for the model's unprepossessing physique. This man is distinctly bony, his knees knobbly, his muscles rather flabby and underdeveloped. But Rembrandt has captured exactly the perspective and the angles of the bones in his model's outstretched leg, and shown how the musculature of the arm appears when being leant on. As with all his seemingly casual studies, even when an anonymous subject is doing nothing in particular, this work is a miracle of observation. This study could become part of the first stage in the planning of a larger composition: the man could equally well be the model for a beggar sitting in the street, or one of the sick brought to Jesus for healing.

In the seventeenth century art students learned by copying: working from existing drawings and plaster casts, before moving on to using live models. The pose of this man resembles that in a contemporary art teaching manual (*A Guide to Drawing and Painting* by Crijspin van de Passe II, 1643). Rembrandt would have intended this pose to test his students' ability at perspective. Close observation and practice were needed to capture accurately the difficult pose of the man's extended leg, as his knee protrudes forward towards the viewer.

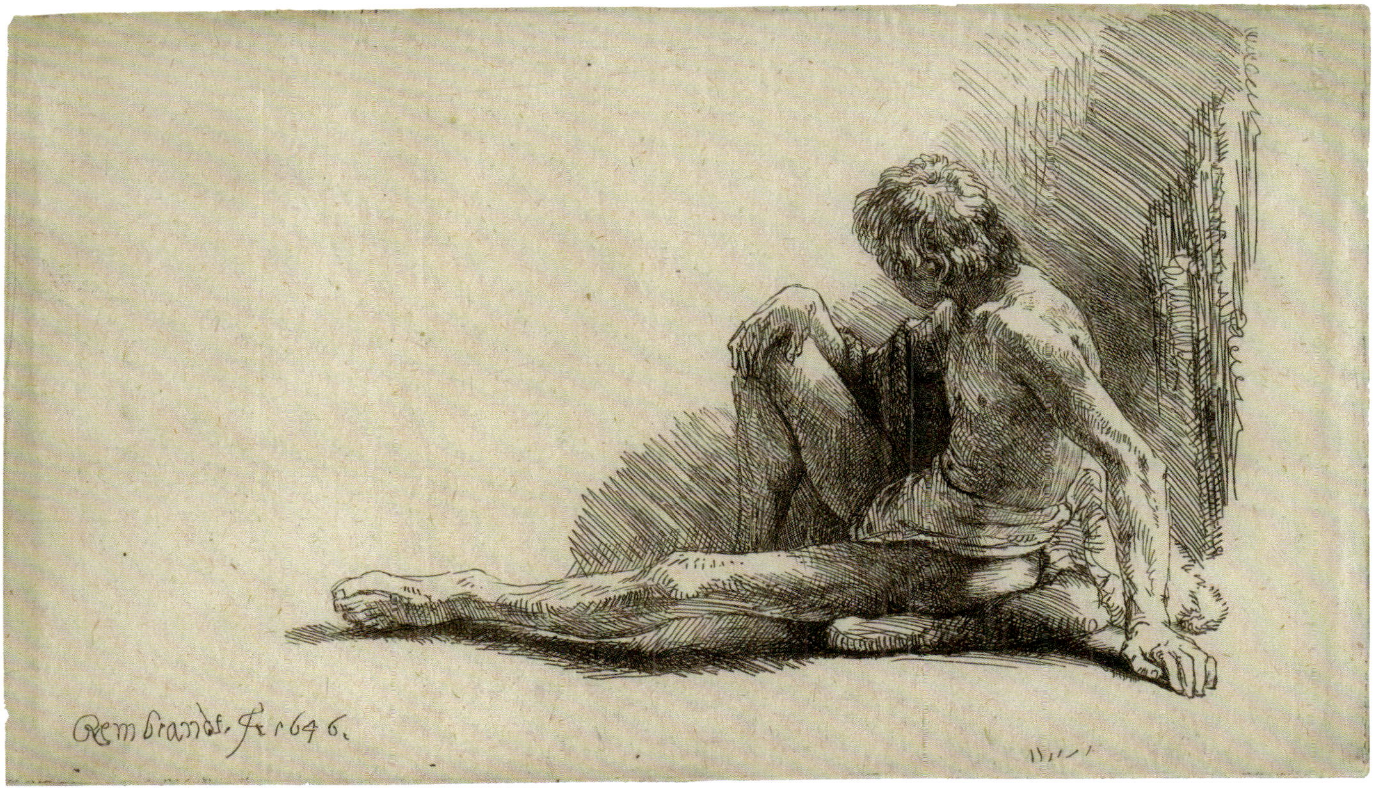
Rembrandt. f. 1646.

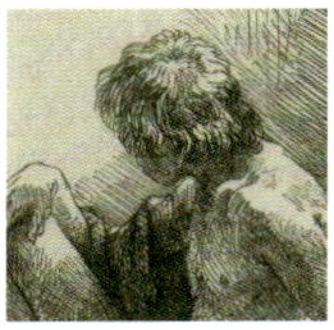

Reclining female Nude ('La Negrèsse Couchée') (IV/VI), 1658
Etching and drypoint on paper
8 x 15.7 cm
Signed and dated in plate lower left of subject 'Rembrandt f. 1658'
NWHCM : 1951.47.92

After 1656, when Rembrandt became bankrupt, all his goods were sold, including his press, and he produced almost no prints after 1658. This same year he also moved out of his large house on the Jodenbreestraat, where he had maintained both a print room and a sizeable painting studio for himself and his students, into a much smaller establishment, where he remained until his death in 1669.

The fourth state of this print is thought to be a posthumous impression, with extra areas of shading and cross-hatching added. Despite its traditional alternative title, current opinion is divided as to whether this beautifully-observed nude is indeed intended to portray a black woman, or a white woman lying in deep shadow in a darkened room. Today, most art-historical opinion inclines towards the latter option.

Ultimately whether she is black or white makes no difference: either alternative would have provided Rembrandt with the artistic and technical challenge of depicting flesh merely as a lighter tone of darkness against the almost completely black background which fills most of the picture. The dark tones of this print make for a lyrical composition, with softer contrasts between the model and her surroundings than any of the other nudes. To depict a reclining nude figure from the back was a familiar artistic subject, but here Rembrandt's dark palette and blurred outlines between flesh and background create a mysterious, highly original interpretation. The effect is one of looking into, almost intruding on, the model's bedroom rather than the public space of a studio: the viewer has the instinct to keep quiet so as not to disturb her sleep.

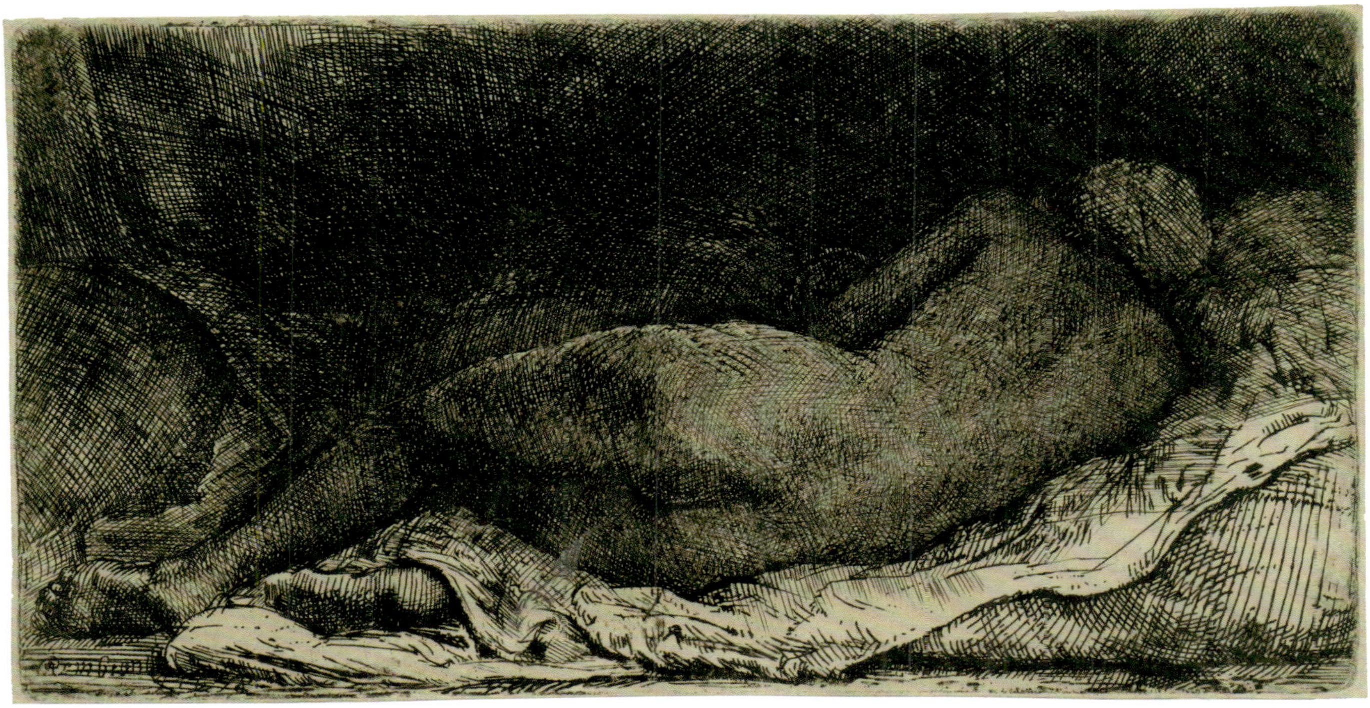

The Norwich Rembrandts

All prints were bequeathed to Norwich Castle Museum & Art Gallery by Percy Moore Turner in 1951. State is supplied after title; dimensions given are for the plate, height x width.

Man Wearing a close Cap, Bust (The Artist's Father?) (VII/VIII), 1630
Etching with touches of drypoint on paper, 7.8 x 6 cm
Signed and dated in plate upper left of subject obscured by later hatching 'RHL 1630', NWHCM : 1951.47.1

Head of a Man in a fur Cap, Crying out (IV/VI), 1629
Etching with touches of drypoint and burin on paper, 3.4 x 2.8 cm
NWHCM : 1951.47.2

The White Negress (III/III), 1630
Etching on paper, 9.8 x 7.8 cm
NWHCM : 1951.47.3

Self-portrait in a heavy Fur Cap, Bust (only state), 1631
Etching on paper, 6.3 x 5.8 cm
Signed and dated in plate upper left of subject 'RHL 1631', NWHCM : 1951.47.4

Naked Woman Seated on a Mound (II/II), 1631
Etching and engraving on paper, 17.7 x 16.1 cm
Signed in plate upper left barely visible monogram 'RHL', NWHCM : 1951.47.5

The Artist's Mother Seated at a Table, Looking right, three-quarter Length (II/III), 1631
Etching on paper, 14.9 x 13.1 cm
Signed in plate lower centre left edge monogram 'RHL. f.', NWHCM : 1951.47.6

The Rat Catcher (III/III), 1632
Etching on paper, 14 x 12.4 cm
Signed and dated in plate lower right of subject monogram 'RHL 1632' ('3' and '2' reversed), NWHCM : 1951.47.7

Self-portrait with raised Sabre (II/II), 1634
Etching with touches of burin on paper, 12.4 x 10.2 cm
Signed and dated in plate upper left 'Rembrandt f. / 1634', NWHCM : 1951.47.8

The Angel Appearing to the Shepherds (III/VI), 1634
Etching, engraving and drypoint on paper, 25.9 x 22 cm
Signed and dated in plate lower right of subject 'Rembrandt f. 1634', NWHCM : 1951.47.9

Christ at Emmaus - The smaller Plate (only state), 1634
Etching and drypoint on paper, 10.2 x 7.3 cm
Signed and dated in plate bottom centre of subject 'Rembrandt f. 1634', NWHCM : 1951.47.10

Self-portrait Wearing a soft Cap, full Face, Head only ('Rembrandt aux trois moustaches') (only state), 1634
Etching on paper, 4.8 x 4.4 cm
NWHCM : 1951.47.11

The Stoning of St Stephen (II/IV), 1635
Etching with touches of burin on paper, 9.5 x 8.5 cm
Signed and dated in plate lower left of subject 'Rembrandt f. 1635', NWHCM : 1951.47.12

Christ before Pilate (IV/V), 1636
Etching and engraving on paper, 55 x 44.8 cm
Signed and dated in plate lower left margin 'Rembrandt f. 1636 cum privile', NWHCM : 1951.47.13

The Pancake Woman (II/VII), 1635
Etching on paper, 10.9 x 7.9 cm
Signed and dated in plate lower centre of subject 'Rembrandt. Ft 1635', NWHCM : 1951.47.14

The Crucifixion, small Plate (I/III), 1635
Etching on paper, 9.5 x 6.7 cm
Signed in plate upper centre 'Rembrandt f.', NWHCM : 1951.47.15

Bald old Man with a short Beard, in Profile right (II/II), 1635
Etching on paper, 6.6 x 5.6 cm
NWHCM : 1951.47.16

Self-portrait with Saskia, Busts (II/IV), 1636
Etching on paper, 10.4 x 9.6 cm
Signed and dated in plate upper left of subject 'Rembrandt. f. / 1636', NWHCM : 1951.47.17

The Return of the Prodigal Son (I/III), 1636
Etching on paper, 15.7 x 13.7 cm
Signed and dated in plate lower centre of subject beneath the two central figures 'Rembrandt f. 1636', NWHCM : 1951.47.18

Young Man in a velvet Cap (II/II), 1637
Etching on paper, 9.6 x 8.3 cm
Signed and dated in plate upper left of subject 'Rembrandt / f 1637', NWHCM : 1951.47.19

Abraham Caressing Isaac (I/IV), 1637
Etching on paper, 11.6 x 8.9 cm
Signed in plate lower left of subject 'Rembrandt f.', NWHCM : 1951.47.20

Three Heads of Women, one lightly Etched (III/III), 1637
Etching retouched with brush and grey ink on paper, 12.7 x 10.2 cm
NWHCM : 1951.47.21

St Catherine ('The little Jewish Bride') (only state), 1638
Etching with touches of drypoint on paper, 11.4 x 7.9 cm
Signed and dated in plate upper right of subject in reverse, very faint 'Rembrandt f: / 1638', NWHCM : 1951.47.22

Self-portrait in a flat Cap and embroidered Dress (I/III), 1642
Etching on paper, 9.2 x 6.3 cm
Signed and dated very faintly upper left 'Rembrandt f.', NWHCM : 1951.47.23

Sheet of Studies, with a Woman ill in Bed (only state), 1639
Etching on paper, 13.8 x 15.2 cm
NWHCM : 1951.47.24

The Death of the Virgin (II/V), 1639
Etching and drypoint on paper, 39.5 x 31 cm
Signed and dated in plate lower left of subject 'Rembrandt f. 1639', NWHCM : 1951.47.25

Death Appearing to a wedded Couple from an open Grave (only state), 1639
Etching and drypoint on paper, 10.9 x 7.8 cm
Signed and dated in plate lower left 'Rembrand [sic] f. 1639', NWHCM : 1951.47.26

Self-portrait Leaning on a Stone-sill (II/II), 1639
Etching with touches of drypoint on paper, 20.5 x 16.4 cm
Signed and dated in plate upper left 'Rembrandt f. / 1639', NWHCM : 1951.47.27

Old Man with a divided fur Cap (I/II), 1640
Etching and drypoint on paper, 14.9 x 13.7 cm
Signed and dated in plate upper left of subject 'Rembrandt f / 1640', NWHCM : 1951.47.28

The Beheading of John the Baptist (I/III), 1640
Etching and drypoint on paper, 12.8 x 10.3 cm
Signed and dated in plate lower left of subject 'Rembrandt f. 1640', NWHCM : 1951.47.29

The Beheading of John the Baptist (III/III), 1640
Etching and drypoint on paper, 12.8 x 10.3 cm
Signed and dated in plate lower left 'Rembrandt f. 1640', NWHCM : 1951.47.30

View of Amsterdam from the Kadijk (only state), 1641
Etching on paper, 11.3 x 15.4 cm
NWHCM : 1951.47.31

Landscape with a Cottage and a large Tree (only state), 1641
Etching on paper, 12.5 x 32 cm
Signed and dated in plate lower right centre 'Rembrandt f 1641',
NWHCM : 1951.47.32

The Windmill (only state), 1641
Etching with touches of drypoint on paper, 14.4 x 20.7 cm
Signed and dated in plate lower right corner 'Rembrandt f 1641',
NWHCM : 1951.47.33

Cornelis Claesz. Anslo, Preacher (III/V), 1641
Etching and drypoint on Japanese paper, 18.6 x 15.7 cm
Signed and dated in plate lower right 'Rembrandt f / 1641', NWHCM : 1951.47.34

Three Oriental Figures (Jacob and Laban?) (II/II), 1641
Etching and drypoint on paper, 14 x 11.3 cm
Signed and dated in plate upper right in reverse 'Rembrandt f / 1641',
NWHCM : 1951.47.35

The Triumph of Mordecai (III/IV), 1641
Etching and drypoint on paper, 17.3 x 21.3 cm
NWHCM : 1951.47.36

Man in an Arbour (only state), 1642
Etching and drypoint on paper, 7.2 x 5.6 cm
Signed and dated in plate upper left 'Rembrandt f 1642', NWHCM : 1951.47.37

The Raising of Lazarus, small Plate (I/I), 1642
Etching with touches of drypoint on oriental paper, 14.9 x 11 cm
Signed and dated in plate lower left of subject figure 2 in reverse 'Rembrandt F / 1642', NWHCM : 1951.47.38

The Descent from the Cross, a Sketch (only state), 1642
Etching and drypoint on paper, 14.9 x 11.6 cm
Signed and dated in plate lower right of subject 'Rembrandt f. 1642',
NWHCM : 1951.47.39

The Hog (II/II), 1643
Etching and drypoint on paper, 14.3 x 15.4 cm
Signed and dated in plate lower right of subject 'Rembrandt f / 1643',
NWHCM : 1951.47.40

The Shepherd and his Family ('Het hardetje') (only state), 1644
Etching and drypoint on paper, 9.5 x 6.7 cm
Signed and dated in plate upper left 'Rembrandt / f 1644', NWHCM : 1951.47.41

The Bridge at Klein Kostverloren on the Amstel, ('Six Bruggetje'), or Six's Bridge (IV/IV), 1645
Etching and drypoint on paper, 13 x 22.4 cm
Signed and dated in plate lower right 'Rembrandt f 1645', NWHCM : 1951.47.42

Abraham and Isaac (I/II), 1645
Etching lightly retouched with pen and grey ink on paper, 15.6 x 12.7 cm
Signed and dated in plate lower left 'Rembrant. [sic] / 1645',
NWHCM : 1951.47.43

The three Trees (only state), 1643
Etching, engraving and drypoint on paper, 21.1 x 28 cm
Signed and dated in plate lower left of subject 'Rembrandt f 1643',
NWHCM : 1951.47.44

Cottages beside a Canal with a View of Ouderkerk (only state), 1641
Etching and drypoint on paper, 14 x 20.7 cm
NWHCM : 1951.47.45

Christ Carried to the Tomb (only state), 1645
Etching and drypoint on paper, 13.1 x 10.6 cm
Signed in plate lower centre of subject 'Rembrant' [sic], NWHCM : 1951.47.46

Nude - Man Seated on the Ground with one Leg Extended (II/III), 1646
Etching and engraving on paper, 9.7 x 16.6 cm
Signed and dated in plate lower left of subject 'Rembrandt. f. 1646',
NWHCM : 1951.47.47

Ephraim Bonus, Jewish Physician (II/II), 1647
Etching, engraving and drypoint on paper, 20.2 x 17.7 cm
Signed and dated in plate lower right of subject 'Rembrandt f 1647',
NWHCM : 1951.47.48

A blind Hurdy-gurdy Player and Family Receiving Alms (I/V), 1648
Etching and drypoint on paper, 16.4 x 12.8 cm
Signed and dated in plate lower right of subject 'Rembrandt f. 1648',
NWHCM : 1951.47.49

Jews in a Synagogue (IV/IX), 1648
Etching and drypoint on paper, 7.1 x 12.9 cm
Signed and dated in plate upper left of subject 'Rembrandt f./1648',
NWHCM : 1951.47.50

Christ with the Sick around Him, Receiving little Children. 'The Hundred Guilder Print' (II/IV), 1648
Etching, engraving and drypoint on paper, 27.8 x 38.9 cm
NWHCM : 1951.47.51

Canal with a large Boat and Bridge ('Het schuytje op de voorgrond') (II/II), 1650
Etching and drypoint on paper, 8.2 x 10.7 cm
Signed and dated in plate lower left of subject 'Rembrandt f. 1650',
NWHCM : 1951.47.52

Landscape with a square Tower (III/III), 1650
Etching and drypoint retouched with pen and grey ink on paper, 8.8 x 15.5 cm
Signed and dated in plate lower right of subject 'Rembrandt f / 1650',
NWHCM : 1951.47.53

Landscape with three gabled Cottages beside a Road (III/III), 1650
Etching on paper, 16.1 x 20.2 cm
Signed and dated in plate lower left of subject 'Rembrandt f 1650',
NWHCM : 1951.47.54

Landscape with a Cow Drinking (II/V), 1650
Etching and drypoint on paper, 10.2 x 12.9 cm
NWHCM : 1951.47.55

View of the Diemerdijk with a Milkman and Cottages ('Het melkboertje') (III/III), 1650
Etching and drypoint on paper, 6.5 x 17.4 cm
NWHCM : 1951.47.56

Clement de Jonghe, Printseller and Artist (VIII/X), 1651
Etching and drypoint on paper, 20.6 x 16.1 cm
Signed and dated in plate lower right of subject 'Rembrandt f. 1651',
NWHCM : 1951.47.57

The Blindness of Tobit: The larger Plate (I/II), 1651
Etching and drypoint on paper, 16.1 x 13 cm
Signed and dated twice in plate lower centre 'Rembrandt f. 1651' and lower right 'Rembrandt f 1651', NWHCM : 1951.47.58

The Flight into Egypt: A night Piece (VI/X), 1651
Etching and drypoint on paper, 12.6 x 11 cm
Signed and dated in plate lower right of subject 'Rembrandt f 1651',
NWHCM : 1951.47.59

The Star of the Kings: A night Piece (I/IV), 1651
Etching with touches of drypoint on paper, 9.4 x 14.3 cm
NWHCM : 1951.47.60

The Star of the Kings: A night Piece (I/IV), 1651
Etching with touches of drypoint on paper, 9.4 x 14.3 cm
NWHCM : 1951.47.61

Cottages and Hay Barn on the Diemerdijk with a Flock of Sheep (II/II), 1650
Etching and drypoint on paper, 8.3 x 17.5 cm
Signed and dated in plate lower left of subject 'Rembrandt f 1650',
NWHCM : 1951.47.62

Cottages and a Hay Barn on the Diemerdijk with a Flock of Sheep (II/II), 1650
Etching and drypoint on paper, 8.3 x 17.5 cm
Signed and dated in plate lower left of subject 'Rembrandt f 1650', NWHCM : 1951.47.63

Christ Disputing with the Doctors: A Sketch (I/II), 1652
Etching and drypoint on paper, 12.6 x 21.4 cm
Signed and dated in plate lower left of subject 'Rembrandt. f. 1652', NWHCM : 1951.47.64

David in Prayer (I/III), 1652
Etching and drypoint on Japanese paper, 14.3 x 9.3 cm
Signed and dated in plate lower left of subject 'Rembrandt f. 1652', NWHCM : 1951.47.65

David in Prayer (II/III), 1652
Etching and drypoint on paper, 14.3 x 9.3 cm
Signed and dated in plate lower left of subject 'Rembrandt f. 1652', NWHCM : 1951.47.66

Cottage with a white Paling (III/III), 1648
Etching and drypoint on paper, 13 x 15.8 cm
Signed in plate lower left centre of subject 'Rembrandt f.', NWHCM : 1951.47.67

Christ Preaching (La Petite Tombe) (I/II), 1657
Etching and drypoint on paper, 15.4 x 20.7 cm
NWHCM : 1951.47.68

Peasant Family on the Tramp (II/III), 1652
Etching on paper, 11.2 x 9.2 cm
NWHCM : 1951.47.69

A Scholar in his Study ('Faust') (I/VIII), 1652
Etching, engraving and drypoint on oatmeal paper, 21 x 16.1 cm
NWHCM : 1951.47.70

Landscape with a Road beside a Canal (only state), 1652
Drypoint on paper, 7.6 x 21.4 cm
NWHCM : 1951.47.71

St Jerome Reading in an Italian Landscape (II/II), 1653
Etching and drypoint on paper, 26 x 20.7 cm
NWHCM : 1951.47.72

The Ringball Player ('Het Klosbaantje'), also known as The Golf Player (I/II), 1654
Etching on paper, 9.6 x 14.4 cm
Signed and dated in plate lower left of subject 'Rembrandt F. 1654', NWHCM : 1951.47.73

The Ringball Player ('Het Klosbaantje'), also known as The Golf Player (II/II), 1654
Etching on paper, 9.6 x 14.4 cm
Signed and dated in plate lower left of subject 'Rembrandt F. 1654', NWHCM : 1951.47.74

The Virgin and Child with the Cat and the Snake (I/IV), 1654
Etching on paper, 9.5 x 14.4 cm
Signed and dated in plate lower centre of subject 'Rembrandt. f. 1654.', NWHCM : 1951.47.75

The Flight into Egypt: Crossing a Brook (only state), 1654
Etching, engraving and drypoint on paper, 9.4 x 14.4 cm
Signed and dated in plate lower left of subject 'Rembrandt f. 1654', NWHCM : 1951.47.76

Christ Seated Disputing with the Doctors (only state), 1654
Etching possibly with touches of drypoint on paper, 9.5 x 14.4 cm
Signed and dated in plate upper left centre of subject 'Rembrandt. f. 1654', NWHCM : 1951.47.77

The Descent from the Cross by Torchlight (I/IV), 1654
Etching and drypoint on paper, 21.1 x 16.1 cm
Signed and dated in plate lower centre left of subject 'Rembrandt. f 1654', NWHCM : 1951.47.78

The Descent from the Cross by Torchlight (III/IV), 1654
Etching and drypoint on paper, 21.1 x 16.1 cm
Signed and dated in plate lower centre left of subject 'Rembrandt. f 1654', NWHCM : 1951.47.79

The Descent from the Cross by Torchlight (I/IV), 1654
Etching and drypoint on paper, 21.1 x 16.1 cm
Signed and dated in plate lower left of subject 'Rembrandt f. 1654.', NWHCM : 1951.47.80

Christ at Emmaus: The larger Plate (IV/V), 1654
Etching and drypoint on paper, 21.1 x 16 cm
Signed and dated in plate lower left of subject 'Rembrandt f. 1654.', NWHCM : 1951.47.81

The Adoration of the Shepherds, with the Lamp (I/II), 1654
Etching on paper, 10.6 x 13 cm
Signed and dated in plate lower left of centre of subject 'Rembrandt. f.', NWHCM : 1951.47.82

The Entombment (Night effect) (IV/IV), 1654
Etching and drypoint on paper, 21.1 x 16.1 cm
NWHCM : 1951.47.83

Christ Presented to the People: Oblong Plate (V/VIII), 1655
Drypoint on vellum, 34.8 x 43.6 cm
NWHCM : 1951.47.84

Abraham's Sacrifice (only state), 1655
Etching and drypoint on paper, 15.6 x 13.1 cm
Signed and dated in plate lower right of subject 'Rembrandt f 1655', NWHCM : 1951.47.85

Pieter Haaringh ('Young Haaringh') (III/VI), 1655
Etching and drypoint on paper, 19.8 x 14.8 cm
Signed and dated in plate in subject bottom of window 'Rembrant [sic] / f 1655', NWHCM : 1951.47.86

Abraham Entertaining the Angels (only state), 1656
Etching and drypoint on paper, 16 x 13.1 cm
Signed and dated in plate lower left of subject 'Rembrandt f. 1656', NWHCM : 1951.47.87

Jan Lutma, Goldsmith (II/V), 1656
Etching, engraving and drypoint on paper, 19.7 x 14.8 cm
Inscribed centre right 'Johannes Lutma Aurifex, / natus Groningae'; signed and dated in plate upper centre of subject on window ''Rembrandt / f. 1656', NWHCM : 1951.47.88

Christ and the Woman of Samaria: An arched Print (III/IV), 1658
Etching and drypoint on paper, 12.4 x 15.8 cm
Signed and dated in plate upper left of subject 'Rembrandt / f. 1658', NWHCM : 1951.47.89

The Agony in the Garden (I/III), 1657
Etching and drypoint on paper, 11.1 x 8.4 cm
Signed and dated in plate lower right of subject 'Rembrandt f. 165...', NWHCM : 1951.47.90

Woman Bathing her Feet at a Brook (I/II), 1658
Etching and drypoint on paper, 15.9 x 8 cm
Signed and dated in plate 'Rembrandt / f. 1658', NWHCM : 1951.47.91

Reclining female Nude ('La Negrèsse Couchée') (IV/VI), 1658
Etching and drypoint on paper, 8 x 15.7 cm
Signed and dated in plate lower left of subject 'Rembrandt f. 1658', NWHCM : 1951.47.92

Lieven Willemsz. van Coppenol, Writing Master: The larger Plate (VII/IX), 1658
Etching, engraving and drypoint on paper, 34.1 x 29 cm
NWHCM : 1951.47.93

Group of Musicians Listening to a Flute Player, 1635
Brown ink and wash on paper, 13.5 x 15.3 cm
Accepted by H.M. Treasury in lieu of estate duty and allocated to Norfolk Museums Service 1978, NWHCM : 1978.184

Summary of printmaking terms

Burin
A v-shaped metal tool used for engraving a plate. Rembrandt sometimes used it to add highlights to a plate already worked in etching or drypoint.

Burr
A sharp drypoint needle leaves displaced metal at the edges of the line it creates when scratched through the metal plate. This displaced metal is called the burr. Burr wears away with use, and fewer impressions can be made from a drypoint plate than from an engraved or etched plate before the line has to be altered or re-made.

Drypoint
For drypoint a sharp needle-like instrument is used to draw straight into the copper plate, creating a burr of fine raised edges. These capture the ink during printing, giving the finished print a characteristic velvety, slightly smudged look very different from the clean lines of straight etching. Rembrandt frequently combined these techniques.

Engraving
A method of intaglio printing. The artist creates the line by cutting directly into a metal plate with a burin.

Etching
Like engraving, a method of intaglio printing. A metal plate is coated with a thin layer of wax, resin and asphalt impervious to acid, known as a 'ground'. The artist draws on this ground with an etching needle, exposing the surface of the plate. The plate is immersed in acid which bites into the exposed areas, the ground is removed and the plate inked and wiped. The ink remaining in the etched lines is transferred onto damp paper using a press.

Impression
A single print from one plate, also called a 'pull'.

State
The different versions of a plate. Some of Rembrandt's prints exist in a single state, for other prints he reworked the plate as many as ten times.

Surface tone
From the 1650s Rembrandt used surface tone, a film of ink deliberately left on the plate before printing. This darkens the subject, achieves greater tonal depth and gives a more painterly effect.

Index